BROOKLANDS
GIANTS

By the same author:

The 200 Mile Race (1947)

The Story of Brooklands, Vol. 1 (1948)

The Story of Brooklands, Vol. 2 (1949)

The Story of Brooklands, Vol. 3 (1950)

The World's Land Speed Record (1951, 1964)

Continental Sports Cars (1951, 1952)

The History of Brooklands Motor Course (1957, 1979)

The Bugatti Story (1960) USA

Montlhéry — The History of the Paris Autodrome (1961)

The Sports Car Pocketbook (1961)

The Vintage Years of the Morgan Three-Wheeler (1970)

Motor Sport Book of the Austin Seven (Editor) (1972)

Motor Sport Book of Donington (Editor) (1973)

The History of Motor Racing (1977)

My 30 Years of Motoring for *Motor Sport* (1982)

Volkswagen Beetle (1982)

Mercedes-Benz 300SL (1983)

Vintage Motor Cars (1985)

Aero-engined Racing Cars at Brooklands (1992)

Black Bess — The Story of an Edwardian Bugatti (1993)

BROOKLANDS
GIANTS

BILL BODDY

Foulis

Haynes

First published in 1995

British Library Cataloguing-in-Publication Data:
A catalogue record for this book is available from
the British Library.

ISBN 0 85429 960 2

Library of Congress catalog card no. 95-77384

Frontispiece: A David Shepherd drawing of John Cobb in the
big Delage winning the close-fought 1932 BRDC British
Empire Trophy race from Captain George Eyston in the 8-litre
Panhard-Levassor, which lost by $^1/_5$th second at the end of the
100 miles. (Reproduced courtesy David Shepherd, this
drawing is available as a limited edition print from the
Brooklands Museum, Weybridge, Surrey KT13 0QN.)

G. T. Foulis & Company is part of
Haynes Publishing,
Sparkford, Nr. Yeovil, Somerset,
BA22 7JJ, England.

Designed & typeset by G&M, Raunds, Northamptonshire
Printed and bound in Great Britain by
Butler & Tanner Ltd, Frome and London

Contents

John Cobb leading in the BROOKLANDS 100 mile race – 1932 Delage
Eyston behind in the Panhard

David Shepherd

Acknowledgements

It is impossible to mention all those who have, over so many years, helped me to acquire specialized information about the racing cars covered in this book.

However, I would like to thank Lord Montagu of Beaulieu for allowing me to use material I wrote for his late-lamented *Veteran & Vintage Magazine*, Alan Chamberlain for much of the information on the Napier L48, and Terence Cuneo, OBE, RGI, for the fine painting used on the dust-jacket which vividly depicts the exciting Match Race at the August Bank Holiday BARC Meeting in 1932 when the red 4½-litre supercharged Bentley single-seater, driven by Sir Henry Birkin, Bt., dramatically caught John Cobb and the old 10½-litre V12 Delage on the run-in to the finish, to win by one-fifth of a second, after lapping at 137.58 mph, the Delage at 133.16 mph. Birkin, entered by the Hon. Dorothy Paget, won 100 sovs for this three-lap race. Also, my thanks to David Shepherd OBE, FRSA, FRGS, for allowing his equally fine drawing of the same driver and Delage battling with Capt. Eyston's 8-litre Panhard-Levassor in that dramatic 1932 BRDC British Empire Trophy race, to be used as the Frontispiece for this book.

I am greatly indebted to all those who have sent me photographs, some of which feature in this book, but whose individual contributions it is impossible to credit after such a long time. However, to all these photographers, including my old friend Guy Griffiths, Helen Lemon who found some of the Benz pictures, the City Museum and Art Gallery in Birmingham who provided others of the Benz in their care, and George E. Wingard and the Long Island Motor Museum for sending me a picture of the 1908 GP Mercedes that is now in the USA, my particular thanks. I am also grateful to Jack and Johnty Williamson for some of the photographs of the 1908 Itala.

And again I thank Mrs Elaine Peberdy for efficiently typing from my execrable copy.

Bill Boddy

Introduction

This is a sequel to my book about the aero-engined monster motor cars that were raced at the Brooklands Motor Course in Surrey, close to the country town of Weybridge, and which enlivened considerably the scene there from 1913 onwards. They contested some of the fastest races held at this, the world's first purpose-built motor track, which had opened in 1907. Exciting cars they certainly were — as I imagine anyone who may have accepted Le Champion's offer in 1928 of a trial run in his 20.5-litre Isotta-Maybach would have agreed, at a time when the car's owner was offering it for sale to the highest bidder!

However, apart from the two aero-powered Sunbeams constructed at the famous Wolverhampton factory in 1913 and just after the Armistice of 1918, respectively, and the great Napier-Railton built within the confines of the Brooklands estate by the engineering firm of Thomson & Taylor Limited (and raced with consummate success from 1933 to 1936) the other aero-engined giants were rather crude devices, in many cases cobbled together by amateurs. I tell of such cars in my book *The Aero-Engined Racing Cars at Brooklands* (Haynes/Foulis, 1992) and since its publication a revival of such hybrids has begun among a keen section of the flourishing Vintage Sports-Car Club.

A Japanese entry for the very first Brooklands Meeting in 1907 — Prince Okura's noisy 120 hp Fiat 'Silver Flyer', which was third behind two Mercedes in the Montagu Cup Race.

But, fascinating as these are, and were, the fact has to be faced that the rest of the giant cars which found their way to the Brooklands Track were much more in the idiom of 'proper' racing cars, built by established automobile manufacturers, and which, when they first emerged from such factories or racing shops, were destined for important road races such as the great French Grand Prix contests, or for establishing course records at the leading European speed-trials and hill-climbs — even for making attacks on the fastest goal of all, the World Land Speed Record. Such cars had, as it were, established themselves on the motor-racing scene before they arrived in Weybridge to thrill the Brooklands spectators, some time after their first flush of mechanical youth.

In the chapters which follow I had to make the difficult decision to limit my descriptions to those cars with engines having a swept volume of 10 litres or over. My assumption was that this was the ordinary person's idea of what constituted a rather awesome and exciting giant among the rest of the competing cars, especially after racing resumed following the end of the First World War. By that time the engine-size of ordinary vehicles was diminishing, and this applied as much to racing cars as to touring machinery. The engine capacity of the competing cars in the 1914 French Grand Prix had been limited to $4^{1}/_{2}$ litres, and after the war the limit fell to 3 litres, then to 2 litres and finally down to $1^{1}/_{2}$ litres; and in modern times it has not risen above $3^{1}/_{2}$ litres. Against this, a racing monster with a power unit of 10 litres or over, particularly if it also possessed the patina of age, held an affectionate fascination for the Brooklands public.

Few catalogue chassis came near to this, if we except as pretty rare birds such models as the ageing Renault 45 (9,120 cc), the Royal Daimlers re-engined with 57 hp (9,421 cc) engines, and the biggest of the six-cylinder Hispano Suizas (7,983 cc) of the kind which Captain Woolf Barnato raced spasmodically at the Track in 1925. I accept at once that the later 8-litre Bentley was much better known, but it is a car very well documented in many other books; and the only time Captain George Eyston ran the slim single-seater 8-litre Panhard-Levassor at Brooklands was in that protest-ridden 1932 BRDC British Empire Trophy outer-circuit race — and the diverse duel he engaged in with John Cobb's $10^{1}/_{2}$-litre Delage is, in any case, covered in Chapter 13 of this book.

So I think my decision was the correct one. After all, a line has to be drawn somewhere, as my publisher will no doubt readily agree! This brings me to the treatment of the Brooklands giants of the pre-First World War era. Ordinary touring cars of that period had much larger engines than was later to be the norm, so that racing cars of the size to which I have applied the under-limit of 10 litres for this book were then less remarkable. That is not to say that the truly big-engined and very fast monsters did not attract the attention of the spectators, and create much excitement. But what would in post-war times, on average, be regarded as 'monster' would then have been much closer to accepted everyday practice, for the small-car invasion had scarcely taken hold by 1912, and in consequence I do not describe *all* those over 10-litre racing cars which before the First World War at Brooklands 'took the cement', as Count Zborowski was later to describe it in his 'Chitty-Bang-Bang' days.

While it is interesting to know that at the very first race meeting at the Brooklands Track on 6 July 1907, huge Mercedes, Napier, Fiat, Darracq and Itala cars did battle, that the Japanese Prince Okura came with his raucous giant 120 hp Fiat, and that very soon Guy Lewin's 80 hp Hotchkiss and McBain's 12-litre De Dietrich 'Saucy Soapbox' and similar giants would grace those pre-1915 BARC entry lists and race-cards, or that L. G. 'Cupid' Hornsted of Big Benz fame would open in 1908 with a large Duplex — unless these drivers and cars appeared in a reasonable number of races with conspicuous success, it would be tedious to list the lot or to add the details of how, for instance, in record-bids Adam Thames did well with a 13,514 cc Thames motor. So I have devoted the earlier chapters to the better-known giants of the pre-WWI period, following with descriptions of all the over-10-litre cars that pleased the crowds after the war, as by then these were distinctly uncommon, had the additional fascination of being old among more recent runners and so stood out among the general run of lesser-sized racing cars. They are in the order in which they first appeared on the entry forms submitted to the Brooklands Automobile Racing Club from 1920 onwards.

The post-war races of the BARC and other clubs were those in which the more conventional giants did battle round the bankings and up the straights with those aero-engined monsters; the average engine capacity of six of the former described hereafter averaged 90.8-litres, compared to an average swept volume of 155.9 for the aeroplane power-units installed in eight of the opposing cars. Yet, in terms of lap-speeds, the former (conventional) giants were only, on average, 1.15 mph slower. I must say I was very sorry, along with many others who favoured the more vintage of the racers, when, for reasons of safety (metal-fatigue and all that), the BARC banned most of these mighty motors after the 1930 season. I hope what follows will stand as a small tribute to those cars which the Brooklands habitués once loved and (silently!) applauded. So, over to some more Heavy Metal . . .

EXPLANATION

To understand properly what follows it is necessary to know something about Brooklands Track, which H. F. Locke King built at his own expense — some £150,000 in the currency of the time (several millions in 1990s val-

Brooklands Track in course of construction — 1906/07.

Brooklands Motor Course in the 1920s. The half-mile Railway Straight is on the right of the picture, the Byfleet banking at the top, the steeper Members' banking in the foreground, with the Finishing Straight running up to meet the latter banking. The Paddock is on the left of the Finishing Straight, and the aeroplane sheds and the sewage farm can be seen in the distance.

ues) — on his estate at Weybridge in Surrey in 1906/7. This concrete-surfaced Motor Course, the very first of its kind in the world, was far from being a 'speed bowl' as sometimes described. Its two curves, the Members' and the Byfleet, were banked to allow drivers to lap, theoretically at 120 mph, with their hands off their steering-wheels. To facilitate this, the bankings were so steep that it was almost impossible for a person to climb up them.

The lower of these banked curves was at the Byfleet side of the course, and this joined the shorter, steeper Members' banking by means of an unbanked reverse-curve at the Fork, where the 991-yards long Finishing Straight ran up to join the main circuit at the foot of the aforesaid Members' banking. This reverse-curve was quite difficult for the faster cars to negotiate. The Track had, in fact, been built on horse-racing lines. The one-acre Paddock — with covered bays for the competitors' cars, a fine Clubhouse and the Telegraph-board — was on the left, going up the straight.

The two banked curves were joined at the eastern side by the half-mile Railway Straight, which ran below the embankment of the L&SWR. The lap distance round the outer-circuit was 2 miles, 1,350 yards. It was over this fast circuit that most of the early Brooklands Automobile Club races were run. In order that all kinds of cars, from stripped sports-cars and specials to old Grand Prix cast-offs and the latest racing cars could compete together, these races were invariably run on a handicap basis, to starting times worked out by the indefatigable Mr A. V. Ebblewhite, based on known performance and practice lap speeds. Most of the giant cars would be heavily handicapped, starting on or close to the scratch mark.

These races were normally divided into Short and Long Handicap contests, the former of around 5³/₄ miles, the latter of about 8¹/₂ miles, with the entries grouped roughly in speed-categories, and the handicapping sorting out the finer divisions. Thus there were 75 mph, 90 mph and 100 mph Short and Long Handicap races, with the very fastest, most exciting cars set to run in the delightfully-named 'Lightning Handicaps'. At first, races finished at the top of the aforesaid Finishing Straight, in view of the Paddock grandstand. But, as the cars became faster, the finishing-line was moved further and further back towards the Fork, to give the drivers more space in which to slow down. Eventually a 'Lightning' finish line was used for the fastest races, but despite this a few cars had gone over the banking because they could not stop in time. So, finally, the finish was transferred to the Railway Straight. The speeds quoted in the following

H. F. Locke King, who built the Brooklands Track on his estate in Weybridge, Surrey, in 1906/07.

A view of the approach to the Members' banking.

chapters are those issued by the official BARC timekeepers.* Further information will be found in my *History of Brooklands Motor Course* (Grenville, London, 1957/1979).

Bill Boddy
Nantmel, Powys 1995

*Brooklands lap-speeds and record-bid average speeds have been compiled from the official records of the Brooklands Automobile Racing Club, endorsed by time-keepers A. V. Ebblewhite and T. D. Duttom, etc., which I am fortunate to have in my possession. If they differ from those in other books this may be because some authors have had to rely on contemporary Press accounts.

1. S. F. Edge's Napiers

With Sunbeam and Wolseley, Napier was one of the British makes to represent Great Britain in motor racing from the early days. From the beginning of Brooklands Motor Course, Stanley Francis Edge, who looked after the interests of the Acton motor manufacturer and was an enormously active publicist for their products (as he was later to be for AC cars), had these Napiers racing and breaking records on the new track.

Indeed, even before the first race meeting on 6 July 1907 Edge had himself set a sensational 24-hour record on the Weybridge course, driving unrelieved for the two rounds of the clock, the track illuminated during the night by road-menders' lanterns and the car's headlamps. Edge thereby gained much publicity for himself, the Napier cars — he was accompanied by two other almost identical ones during his epic drive — and for

The fastest car in S. F. Edge's team of Brooklands Napiers, the famous 'Samson', with Frank Newton at the wheel. Note the coolant tubes round the nose and sides of the bonnet.

Cecil Edge and 'Samson', known officially as L48.

the new Brooklands Track. However, the Napiers used were 60 hp six-cylinder models of 7,676 cc (5 in. x 4 in. bore and stroke) — an engine size below that which I have set for this book.

Pre-Brooklands — the 90 hp Napier at the Bexhill speed trials.

Among these different Napiers which formed Edge's Brooklands' team, was the remarkable six-cylinder two-speed L48, built for the 1904 Gordon Bennett race with a 15-litre engine and subsequently enlarged to a final

capacity of over 20 litres. By then known as 'Samson' and famed as having taken part in the 1908 Match Race against the Fiat, it was a sensationally quick car for its day and age, having reached 130 mph at Brooklands that same year and been timed officially at 119.34 mph over the kilometre.

The first competitive run for L48 was in the September 1904 speed trials at Portmarnock Sands. It put up fastest time. Its next appearance — also in September — was at Gaillon hill-climb in France. Although the Napier speed was 76 mph up the 1-in-10 gradient it was, at that stage of development, not quite fast enough to beat the larger-engined cars of Gobron-Brille and Darracq; they were both just 0.4 of a second faster. Taken to Ormond-Daytona beach in Florida, USA, in January 1905, the Napier was successful in setting important world records — the Standing Kilometre 27.2 seconds (81.6 mph); the Flying Kilometre 23 seconds (97.26 mph); the Flying Mile 34.4 seconds (104.65 mph); five miles at 91.37 mph; ten miles at 96 mph (Winning the 'Thomas' Trophy). All these records were achieved with the Daytona beach sand in rippled condition, which may account for variations in speed for some of the short-distance records. The six-cylinder Napier had established itself as the world's fastest car. It had also displayed a characteristic of the high-powered cars of the period — it could accelerate quickly and attain its maximum speed in quite a short distance, after which the speed dropped off. Although L48 had only a two-speed gearbox, to meet speed and weight requirements with the length of a six-cylinder power unit, it showed outstanding acceleration for the period. All photos of its standing start contests taken at the time show the Napier well out ahead in the first 1/4 mile — even ahead of the Stanley Steamer which had stored energy built up in its high-pressure steam before starting to move off.

The next appearance of Napier L48 was on the Isle of Man in March for the eliminating trials to select the British team for the 1905 Gordon Bennett race to be held near Clermont-Ferrand in France. The six-cylinder Napier L48, as expected, proved by a big margin to be the fastest car. However, it suffered some problems during the 311 miles of racing over the hilly and difficult Isle of Man course. There was some gear selector trouble, the guard over the exposed water pump drive chain became damaged, causing the chain to break, and finally the handbrake locked on causing driver Arthur MacDonald to lose control at Ramsay and hit a stone wall. This accident was caused by poor design of the brake linkage, and one of the four cylinder cars had suffered a similar problem at earlier trials.

The six-cylinder L48 was not seriously damaged and, as it had proved to be by far the fastest British car, it was selected to run in the 1905 Gordon Bennett race. Close up photos taken at the time, showing details of construction, indicate that the car was poorly prepared for this difficult 340-mile race over the Auvergne circuit. Although timed over a kilometre in the race as the fastest car, the Napier finished a poor ninth. The fuel tank fell off, losing the petrol, and new supplies had to be bought after the tank had been lashed back into position. The seat became detached and the engine is said to have stopped on many occasions. As re-starting involved strenuous efforts on the handle by both driver and mechanic, a lot of time was lost. The best that can be said of the Napier performance in the 1905 Gordon Bennett was that it was driven from the factory to the course, showed highest speed, completed the contest and was driven home under its own power. The race was won by Léon Théry, driving a Richard Brasier.

During 1905 the six-cylinder Napier ran in many English events and usually put up fastest time. At the seafront contests at Brighton on a road section measuring 80 yards short of a mile followed by minimal stopping distance, it ran 45.2 seconds from a standing start (79.5 mph) and established a British record for the Flying Start Kilometre at 97.2 mph. At Blackpool in July it ran at 104.52 mph over the flying kilometre and 96.25 mph for the mile, easily beating the 100 HP Fiat and the 100 HP Darracq over this course. In late 1905 Clifford Earp took the Napier to the Château Thierry hill-climb in France and made fastest time of the day. Taken to the speed trails on the road at Dourdon, France, the Napier made fastest time of the day over both the kilometre and mile.

In January 1906 the Napier was again taken across the Atlantic for speed trials on Ormond-Daytona beach, but on this occasion the Stanley steam car was able to do 127.66 mph over the mile, and no internal combustion-engined car of the period could even approach this speed. The Stanley's record speed was not exceeded in Europe for 15 years. However, the steam car could hold its speed only over short distances, and the Napier won the five-mile race and the 100-mile race for the Minneapolis Cup.

In October 1906 the Napier, now getting obsolete, ran at the Blackpool speed trials in competition with the 200 hp V8 Darracq and other cars, but had to accept second fastest time to the Darracq. However, the Napier, driven by Miss Dorothy Levitt, established a ladies' record with two runs at 90.9 mph.

In July 1907 Brooklands racing track was opened at Weybridge in

The 15-litre engine of the Napier L48 as it was raced at Brooklands in 1907.

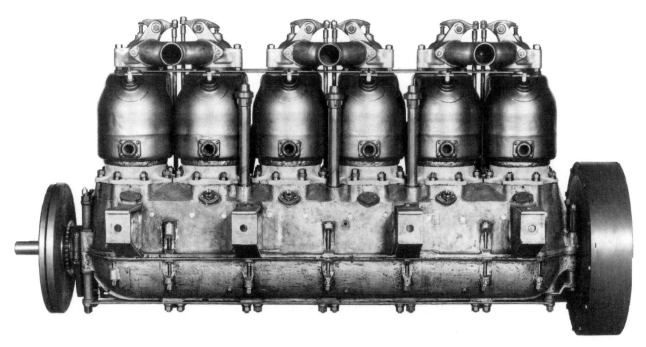

Surrey, and S. F. Edge established a team of six-cylinder Napier cars covering a range of different powers for competing in the various classifica-
tions. Of these cars L48 had the largest engine capacity of 15-litres and
was the only car built completely as a racing machine. The other cars were
modified from production Napiers of different models. All these cars,
including L48, had a successful season, netting a total of £1,700 in prize
money.

Late in 1907, Newton (Napier's works driver) took L48 to Gaillon hill-
climb (its fourth visit) and put up the fastest time of the day at 26.6 sec-

*The inlet side of the
Napier's engine.*

*The exhaust side of the
Napier's engine.*

How it all started — the three 7.7-litre Napiers which undertook the epic 24-hour run at Brooklands in 1907, which effectively opened the new Track. S. F. Edge drove the lead car, supported by the other two 60 hp Napier.

onds (84 mph). This was 2.5 seconds better than the car had previously achieved on the hill.

At the Easter Meeting in 1908, Newton vanquished Dario Resta's 76 hp Mercedes, after L48 had slipped down the wet banking into the German car. They touched briefly, but both drivers kept control, although the Mercedes had a dented hub cap and the Napier, which won at 89.5 mph, had several spokes torn from its nearside wire wheels!

Early in 1908, L48 was fitted with a new engine having a smaller cylinder bore of $6\frac{1}{8}$ in. (to come within the 90 hp RAC rating) but a longer stroke of 6 in. (155x152 mm) and was now known as 'Samson'. It remained in this form until almost mid-1908.

Also early in 1908, Newton, with one of the 90 hp Napiers (see later), had taken the 90 hp class half-mile record (a distance observed by the Brooklands ARC) from Dario Resta's 76 hp Mercedes at a speed of 102.85 mph, compared to the Mercedes' 95.5 mph. The highlight of the 1908 Whitsun meeting was a challenge race between 'Samson' and a specially-built four-cylinder 18,145 cc Fiat racing car known as 'Mephistopheles'. This Fiat was driven by Felice Nazzaro, and the Napier by Frank Newton.

Some of the other successful cars of Edge's Napier team, although all under 10-litres capacity. Tryon is in the car in the top right picture, and Newton is in the driving seat in the other two photographs — all taken in the Brooklands Paddock in Edwardian times.

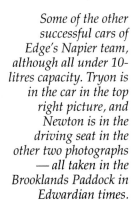

For the race the Napier had been fitted with a new crankshaft giving a piston stroke of 7 in. and a displacement of over 20 litres. This engine is stated to have developed 212 bhp at 2,500 rpm — a high speed for such an engine.

The cars were started from a position 490 yards from the timing strip, so it was something of a flying start, and the Napier was 19 seconds ahead of the Fiat when they crossed the strip. Newton maintained a substantial lead until near the end of the third lap when a big-end bolt broke and he was forced to retire. He drove the Napier very carefully back to the paddock (contemporary reports referred to a melted bearing or a broken crankshaft). A new electrical-timing device had been installed at Brooklands Track and it credited the Fiat with its second lap at 121.64 mph and the Napier's best lap at 113.01 mph. The Napier was leading until it had to retire and, at the time, neither car could seemingly lap at a speed approaching that recorded by the electrical timing device. Hand timing by experts credited the Fiat with 108 mph and 'Samson' with a best lap of 105.7 mph, but the tapes from the timing device were sent to the RAC, whose Competitions Committee declared themselves satisfied.

In attempts to solve the mystery, many theories have been put forward. Obviously the electrical timing strip could not discriminate between the Napier and the Fiat, and would be manually triggered for each car. It would accurately measure the period between each time a car passed over it, but somebody had the responsibility for triggering the device which indicated which car it was. It is likely that in the excitement of the moment some wrong buttons were pressed by the timing device operator. The Fiat remained at Brooklands for some weeks attacking Class records held by 'Samson', but was not able to equal them.

At the August 1908 Brooklands Meeting 'Samson', driven by Frank Newton, won the 30-mile race for the Montagu Cup at 101.5 mph, which constituted a new record, beating Lane's 76 hp Mercedes and Resta's 60 hp Mercedes. In October, Newton, with 'Samson', raised the 90 hp ten-lap record to 102.21 mph and the half-mile record to 114.98 mph. Perhaps the crowning achievement in the career of both Frank Newton and 'Samson' was at their last appearance at Brooklands on 18 November 1908 when the 90 hp Class Short Record was pushed up to 119.34 mph. Running the reverse way of the track the big six-cylinder car reached 130 mph on the Byfleet banking. It will be realized that tyre life and road or track conditions were the limiting factors at this period, rather than absolute top speed of the cars. This, of course, applied to cars of all makes.

There is no sufficiently detailed information available to establish the exact date of each of the many modifications made to the chassis and engine of the famous Napier, but their sequence can be related to dated photographs. When the car was first seen in June 1904 it had obviously been rushed through to make the earliest possible showing. The separate small reverse gear lever was not installed, and the top leaves of the front springs were too short to give the shackles a workable angle. First modification was the fitting of longer top leaves to the front springs. The next obvious change was replacing the temporary flat radiator with a cooling system using unfinned copper tubes running horizontally from a pointed tank at the front right along both sides of the engine. The drawing of this modification — one of the few modification drawings located — is dated '27-5-04', so this unusual cooling system was designed but not installed before the car was shown. S. C. H. ('Sammy') Davis, the famous motoring writer who was around in those early days, said that the distinctive cooling system was fitted on instructions from S. F. Edge to give the car a unique appearance rather than to improve cooling efficiency. The fact that the horizontal tube system has no particular engineering merit, and restricts accessibility, lends weight to this view. This cooling system does give the car a brutish but attractive appearance, and from an observer's view sets it out apart from any other car.

The next modification was the installation of a speedometer — at first friction driven by an aluminium cone attached to the offside front wheel hub engaging a leather-faced cone on a spring loaded spindle connecting to the flexible drive cable. This system was soon replaced by a spur gear drive in the same location. Around March 1905 Dunlop built some non-detachable wire wheels suitable for use on a powerful car, and the Napier was fitted with this equipment to replace the wood-spoked type. During the successful record runs in January 1905 at Daytona Beach in Florida, MacDonald had experienced some steering problems, presumably caused by the very short torque tube inducing rear-wheel steering when even a small amount of side-sway occurred on the rear springs. For the Gordon Bennett race a major change was made in the method of mounting the rear axle. Radius rods were now fitted to take the axle thrust and to retain correct alignment for more accurate steering.

The ratchet pawl and mechanism was removed from the handbrake lever to prevent recurrence of accidents which had been caused by the brake locking on. The faulty geometry which caused the problem was never corrected.

Some of the excess 'camber' was taken out of the front springs in 1906, but no further noticeable changes were made to the chassis until 1907. The opening of Brooklands Racing Track in July 1907 provided opportunities to run the Napier at high speed over the relatively short race distances, and also to set up British records. By this time Rudge Whitworth had developed their detachable wire wheel, held in position by a central locking ring screwed to the hub. These newly-developed wheels were fitted to the Napier, and shortly after this a more robust front axle was fitted. Drum type friction shock absorbers were installed, and this necessitated alterations to the steering layout. The front steering arm had originally been fitted above the axle beam but was now moved to a position below the axle to give space for the shock absorbers to link to the widely spaced U-bolts for the springs. The springs were now altered to provide a flat top leaf, and to maintain chassis height much longer shackles were fitted. Putting the steering arm below the axle permitted the use of a straight drag link in place of the earlier design which had to curve around the spring to permit clearance when the wheels were locked over. The lower position at the front of the drag link, however, provided poor steering geometry which was made still worse when later the Pitman arm at the steering box was reduced in length to give the driver more leverage.

These steering modifications would accentuate the tendency to 'wheel fight', but the car lived with this situation for the remainder of its life. Around this time the radius rods locating the rear axle were deleted, and no definite information is available on how the axle thrust was then taken. There is some evidence that the rear shackles were locked up when the car was nearing the end of its useful life. For Brooklands racing in 1908 the bolster tank was removed and a rectangular fuel tank installed where the bucket seat for the passenger had originally been. As there was no longer a requirement for the car weight to be below 1,000 kg, it was desirable to make several modifications. A new cooling system header tank was installed on brackets at the front of the chassis. This new tank replaced the long narrow tank which had been fed by simple vertical rubber pipes and was mounted along the top of the engine. The new header tank was a well-finished job and of pleasing shape, and it improved the appearance and permitted the use of a simple straight bonnet. It was later replaced by a tank of generally similar shape but crudely made. This change could have been necessitated by an accident or a fatigue failure.

Some months later a new engine was fitted. This engine was of the same basic layout as the original but was of smaller bore ($6\frac{1}{8}$ in.) but longer stroke (6 in.) than the earlier power unit. A new crankshaft, providing 7 in. stroke, was fitted in time for the famous match with the Fiat at Whitsun 1908. The new engine had an improved lubricating system and valve action, permitting it to be run-up to a very high piston speed for the period.

After Edge had abandoned racing, L48 was sold and its lightweight chassis, in poor condition, was broken up. Both the first 15-litre engine and the 20-litre power unit fitted in 1908 went into speed-boats. The smaller engine was purchased from Edge by Perch Cornwall of Melbourne, Australia, and used to power the Cornwalls' *Nautilus II*, said to be the fastest boat in Australia at the time, but early in 1916 the Napier engine was replaced by an American V8 aero-engine. In its Napier-powered form *Nautilus II* had won many races, including the Griffiths Cup event for unlimited-size boats in 1914 and again in 1915, beating the famous French Richard-Brasier boat imported specially for this event by Anthony Hordern of Sydney. The Cornwall brothers then went off to the war in Europe, leaving the 1904 Napier racing-car engine in a corner of their pottery works. There it stayed until 1950 when that great enthusiast and capable engineer, the late Alan ('Bob') Chamberlain, discovered it. Having identified it as the original $6\frac{1}{4}$ in.-bore engine from L48, as designed by the talented A. W. Rowledge, Napier's Chief Engineer, who later designed the successful Napier 'Lion' aero-engine before joining Rolls-Royce. Chamberlain decided to make a replica chassis for the engine following faithfully the original chassis in all but a few details. Thus he based his work on the car as raced at Brooklands in 1908, with its remarkable radiator tubes flanking its bonnet, but retaining the bolster petrol tank and two bucket seats used when the car was raced earlier on road circuits.

Chamberlain, being an honest man, didn't hide the fact that this was a replica. He made no secret of how, in building it, he had slightly departed from L48's chassis as it was from 1904 to 1908, but he kept the engine as close to the original specification as possible. As it was, about the only changes in design to the replica chassis were that the diameter of the brake drums for the rear wheels was increased from 8 in. x $1\frac{1}{2}$ in. to 11 in. x $2\frac{1}{4}$ in. to match the dimensions of the transmission brake, the small size of the original drums having been dictated by the need to meet the minimum weight of below 1,000 kg imposed by the regulations of the race for which L48 was first intended. Also, to save making masses of special ones, the early Whitworth bolts were not copied, and instead modern fine and coarse threaded ones with the 60° standard angle were used. The chassis length was increased by 2½ in. to accommodate a vibration damper on the engine's crankshaft, fitted to obviate possible breakage from the vibration the engine had suffered from; and various sets of wheels were made up, to take headed-edge and modern-type tyres.

Alan ('Bob') Chamberlain, who made a magnificent job of building a replica of the Napier L48 in Australia in recent times, having discovered the original 15-litre engine (which had been used to power a speed boat), which he also meticulously rebuilt. He is seen with the 5 ft. 7 in.-long crankshaft, forged from a steel billet.

The late Alan ('Bob') Chamberlain in happy mood in his recreation of the famous Napier 'Samson'.

The creditable rebuild was completed only after Alan Chamberlain had come to England to study Napier drawings held in London's Science Museum, and to consult such Napier experts as Ronald ('Steady') Barker, Anthony Heal and Frank Johnson, etc. The work was facilitated for Bob, who was then over 70, by his former Chamberlain Industries Company,

A rear view of the replica of the Napier which was one of Brooklands' most famous and fastest cars in the early days of the Track.

now Chamberlain John Deere, which had been the main source of aluminium alloy castings for the Australian Motor Industry and whose Rolloy Piston Company had provided it with pistons of all kinds. It was completed by July 1982, when the engine was started-up. That September the car was proudly demonstrated at Australia's Sandown race meeting, using a 3-to-1 axle ratio, which limited speed on the 880x120 tyres, since they were prone to move on the rims, shearing the inner tubes. At the Geelong seafront speed trials in November, Chamberlain covered the standing-start 1/4-mile in 16.9 seconds (after a cautious start to preserve the tyres) but, in pulling up, the Napier ran up the kerb, resulting in burst tyres and damage to the brake gear. A 1.85-to-1 axle was then fitted and the tyres changed for 21x6.00 ones. On a chassis dynamometer the engine gave 180 bhp, but the tyres would only stand this for two minutes.

Shared with Tony Gaze, the Napier was driven at Mangalore airstrip in April 1983, and timed by the VSCC of Australia at around 100 mph. It was sent to England in May and was demonstrated at Donington Park, and at Brooklands, where members of the Brooklands Society were delighted to see the replica L48 in action on part of the Members' banking, much in the trim it would have been in for the first BARC season of 1907, but with the side-tube radiator that will forever be associated with 'Samson' in 1908. The car was then taken to Shelsley-Walsh in July 1983, where Bob, although cornering carefully so as not to shed a tyre, completed the hill-climb in 50.4 seconds. Finally, it participated in the VSCC Colerne speed trials, where, using 21x7.00 rear tyres and with Gaze driving, the car did the standing-start kilometre in 30.67 seconds (with a timed terminal speed of 111.73 mph), and the owner did a time of 31.22 seconds, and a terminal velocity of 109.29 mph. After this the Napier was exhibited in Tom Wheatcroft's Donington Park Racing Car Museum before returning to Australia. Alan Chamberlain had considered giving his splendid replica

C. A. Bird's Napier competing at Beacon Hill in 1911, where it made fastest climb of the day.

to the Brooklands Museum in England, but just prior to his death he decided it should stay in Australia. I am indebted to much of Bob's meticulous research for the above notes.

Reverting to the original Napiers of S. F. Edge's day, a second 90 hp (155×102 mm) was built, rather heavier than L48 and known as 'Meteor', with a standard Type 120 chassis. It was only run once at Brooklands, when Frank Newton brought it out at that eventful Whitsun 1908 Meeting, and in the five-mile '90 hp Stakes' vanquished Dario Resta's 76 hp (RAC rating) Mercedes, going along the Railway Straight at 115 mph and winning by 200 yards at 91 mph. Later, Newton drove it at Saltburn Sands, where it covered the flying-start kilometre at 102.6 mph.

Most of the Edge Napiers were cars of under 10 litres, and so outside the scope of this book, but an exception was the long-stroke 65 hp car (5 in. × 6 in. bore and stroke) which that versatile driver C. A. Bird (of the Bird's Custard Powder company) bought from S. F. Edge and drove at the Track during 1910, heavily handicapped in the 'All Comers' Plate' race of 100 sovs, in which he lapped at 87.34 mph, taking third place in a 1911 Private Competitors' Handicap and the same placing in a Sprint event at the Track. Afterwards the car was bought in 1914 by Major Sholto Wilson, who used it as a fast road-going car until 1923, by which time he felt that as its stopping distance, especially on wet roads, was not the equal of that of four-wheel-braked cars, he had better lay it up. It was put into a shed at Greywell in Hampshire. During World War II Denis Jenkinson came to hear of this and, in 1949, I was able to introduce it to Ronald ('Steady') Barker, who was then running a 1909 Napier but had always wanted one of the big six-cylinder Napiers. After Major Wilson's death in 1962 he was able to purchase the Sixty and completely overhaul it. It then became one of the VSCC's more outstanding Edwardians, appearing in many of their events, until Barker sold it to Trevor Tarring and Tony Jones, who continued to make much-appreciated appearances in it.

2. The 200 hp V8 Darracq

The V8 200 hp Darracq never competed in a Brooklands race, but I feel I must include it, because it was an exceedingly exciting motor car and because it was very fast by the standards of 1907. It also had the largest capacity engine of any car to take the Weybridge cement, except for the aero-engined monsters. Alexandre Darracq had gained the coveted Land Speed Record in 1904 when Barras drove one of his cars to a speed of 104.52 mph at Ostend. It was presumably to defend this title against all comers that the French manufacturer had built the fabulous 200 hp V8 racing car.

It was certainly a fearsome creation. Using two cylinder blocks from the 1904 'Vanderbilt Cup' Darracqs set at 90° on a common crankcase, with forked connecting rods, an engine of 160×140 mm bore and stroke (22,518 cc) was obtained. The former side exhaust valves were lifted to an overhead location, all the valves being operated by long push-rods and enor-

The extremely fast and exciting 1905 200 hp V8 Darracq, which never raced at Brooklands but was not unknown there.

mous rockers, from a camshaft in the centre of the crankcase. All this impressive valve gear was fully exposed. There were eight stub exhaust pipes, four per side, and two carburettors fed the cylinders. There was nothing much else.

This enormous power unit was mounted in a flimsy chassis with a wheelbase of only 8 ft. 6 in. A big water tank with a pointed prow was carried above the engine, supplementing a sharply V-shaped gilled-tube radiator. There were two shallow bucket seats and a small cylindrical petrol tank behind them. Two speeds sufficed in the shaft-drive transmission — and that was the 200 hp Darracq. The engine, the work of Ribeyrolles, was said to develop 200 bhp at 1,200 rpm, and the car weighed only 19¼ cwt. At Daytona a Napier had gone fractionally quicker than the earlier Darracq (although its speed was not recognised in Europe), and Hemery took the 200 hp car to the Arles–Salon road just after Christmas 1905 and lifted the official LSR to 109.65 mph. This was just too late to have been a welcome Christmas present for M. Darracq.

At this point the Hon. (later Sir) Algernon Lee Guinness of the Guinness brewery family, bought the big Darracq. In this he was no doubt aided because he had driven for Darracq in the important races of the time. First, however, he drove the car at the Gaillon hill-climb in France, making best time in 1905 at 89.47 mph and in the Ostend speed-trials in July 1906, where he covered the kilometre at 117.7 mph.

At Skegness that September Algernon Lee Guinness gave a demonstration run on the sands at the Notts AC races. During the month following, the Darracq was put on a train hired by the more wealthy drivers, who

Sir Algernon Guinness, Bt., who in earlier times had tamed the fearsome 200 hp V8 Darracq.

The fate of the 200 hp Darracq — its chassis was used by Oscar Morris for racing at Brooklands with a Daimler engine installed.

dined in style in the restaurant coach as their cars were taken to Blackpool, where A. Lee Guinness at first tied with Cecil Edge's 90 hp Napier but then topped his speed, against a strong headwind, by 2½ mph, thereby establishing a world standing-start kilometre record of 32.4 seconds, and won two races, the flying-start unlimited event at 103.4 mph.

In 1907 A. Lee Guinness was still running the V8 Darracq to great effect. At the Yorkshire AC's Saltburn speed-trials he devoured the flying-start kilometre at 111.84 mph, recognized as the 'Yorkshire Record' for sand racing, and in June 1908 he took the car to the same venue and was timed over the flying-start kilometre at 121.57 mph, a record not beaten until 1922, and then unofficially. Newton's 90 hp Napier had been 18.96 mph below this speed. On this epoch-making run the riding mechanic was his brother, K. Lee Guinness, who after the war was to become famous as the driver of Louis Coatalen's big V12 Sunbeam and his 'Invincible' 1½-litre Darracqs.

Presumably the car was considered too difficult or frail to race at Brooklands, but when an American, Mr Dugald Ross, said he would buy the Darracq for £2,000 if it proved sufficiently fast to satisfy him, A. Lee Guinness took him to Brooklands where, timed by the American and a friend, a distance of 20 chains was done at 112.2 mph, and then at 115.4 mph. The BARC must also have timed the Darracq officially, because the first two BARC Certificates ever issued were given for these performances. Remembering that in 1908 the Fiat 'Mephistopheles' during the famous Match Race against the 90 hp Napier 'Samson' was timed to do a lap at 121.64 mph by the new electrical apparatus but at only 107.98 mph by the probably more-reliable (at that time) hand timing, suggesting a top pace of around 118 mph, the speed of the Darracq the year before is certainly impressive.

However, the deal fell through; Mr Ross seems to have ridden on the car and perhaps the experience was more than he had bargained for! But this establishes the 22.5-litre Darracq as the car with the largest non-aero

The Oscar Morris Daimler in a later form, with more streamlined bodywork.

engine to use the Brooklands Motor Course — and now, I suppose, someone is going to remind me that Darracq also made aeroplane engines!

The ageing Darracq was still serving A. Lee Guinness well in 1909, when it did 120.25 mph over Saltburn's flying-start kilometre (the fastest of the 1908 GP Mercedes cars was over 27 mph slower). Soon after this it was deemed wise to stop, for the flimsy chassis had no doubt done enough. However, the big Darracq had made a great impression when Guinness first acquired it, not least according to H. W. Bunbury, who described how Lord Annesley had told Algy that the Darracq was for sale in Oxford Street, to where they proceeded in His Lordship's unsilenced Mercedes Sixty. They found the 200 hp car in a basement, where it was started up, 'tis said, creating an inferno of noise, smoke, flames and fumes. It was towed to Datchet behind the Mercedes, and the Guinness brothers used to test it at dawn on the Hartfordbridge Flats, near Camberley, with friends guarding side-roads and the police sometimes interested onlookers. From rides in the mechanic's seat Bunbury, who was used to early racing cars, says that nothing else matched a full throttle run on the '200' for a real thrill and for pure joy, with the car in Algy's capable hands. Riding on the 200 hp Darracq must have been an alarming experience, because there was very little for the passenger to hang on to, and neither he nor the driver had any protection from the engine or flywheel, as no bulkhead was fitted. Guinness did take the car to Brooklands on one more occasion, to tune it up before the Saltburn speed trials. In the end the chassis was disposed of to Oscar Morris, who installed therein a poppet-valve 8-litre Daimler engine, adding a rather cumbersome body and a Spyker-like radiator and bonnet, and in 1914 won two races, with a lap speed of over 87½ mph — so at least part of the famous V8 Darracq raced on the Track!

Sir Algernon Guinness kept the engine from the big Darracq until his death in October 1954, after which it passed into the hands of VSCC-member G. D. Firkins, who still has it.

3. The Fiat 'Mephistopheles'

Fiat had a particularly successful road racing season in 1907, including victory in the French Grand Prix, which Felice Nazzaro had won at 70.5 mph with a four-cylinder 180×160 mm car. It was, no doubt, these successes that caused Sir George Abercromby, Bt., a Guards officer who lived in Aberdeenshire, to place an order for a special Fiat that would be capable of 116 mph and be able to win the 1908 Montagu Cup race at Brooklands. The agreed price was £2,500.

This car was duly put in hand. Not a great deal of technical information is available about this famous Fiat which arrived in England during the summer of 1908 and, driven by the great Nazzaro, won the Match Race for 20 sovs a side against the challenger, Newton, driving S. F. Edge's 90 hp Napier 'Samson'. Nazzaro averaged 94.75 mph for the 27.25 miles, and the Fiat's fastest lap was at 107.98 mph by hand-timing, and 121.64 mph by the BARC's electrical timing apparatus — to this day controversy rages as to which was correct, but Nazzaro had accomplished what was expect-

The Grand Prix Fiat of 1907, on which 'Mephistopheles' was closely based.

ed of him, and returned to Italy richer by £700 (his fee was £500 and the English Fiat Company gave him a present of £200, an enormous sum by today's values and in terms of current starting money).

The Fiat, commonly referred to as 'Mephistopheles', had a four-cylinder engine rated at 89.5 hp. The actual dimensions are obscure. The cylinder bore was 190 mm. Laurence Pomeroy has given it as 140 mm, and in 1913, at Brooklands, it was officially published as 185 mm. But, in 1922, after it had been idle for many years, Captain John Duff presumably stripped the engine down before racing it, and he certainly had the 'pots' off when installing lightweight pistons, so he had an opportunity to measure it. Thus I accept these dimensions, (190×160mm) which give a capacity of 18,145 cc.

The cylinders were cast in pairs, with, according to *The Motor*, two exhaust valves per cylinder, actuated by a common push-rod, on the near-side and one inlet valve per cylinder on the offside, the rockers across the heads clearing one another by a very narrow margin. The camshaft was in the base chamber on the offside, driven by exposed timing pinions, from which another spur gear drove the magneto of the low-tension ignition system. The valves were in cages some 4 in. in diameter. Cooling was by pump, but there was no fan, and the honeycomb radiator was of typical Fiat shape. The lubrication system incorporated a dashboard oil-box and belt-drive dredger pump.

The great Felice Nazzaro, who was to win the celebrated Fiat/Napier Match Race at Brooklands in 1908, after winning the 1907 French GP at Dieppe on a similar Fiat.

The chassis followed Fiat GP design, the drive going via a plate clutch, and final drive being by side chains. The side-members were undrilled, suspension was by half-elliptic springs, and there was no body apart from two bucket seats, the long steering column being unsupported. The external gear and brake levers and the driving sprockets were drilled for lightness (or smart appearance) and the right-hand pedal applied a metal-to-metal

NAZZARO, Vainqueur du Grand Prix de l'A. C. F. sur Voiture Fiat

shoe brake on the front of the gearbox and another brake on the offside of the differential shaft. Artillery 12-spoke wooden wheels were used, those at the back having heavy ornamental spokes. A big exhaust pipe fell away to a huge tail pipe on the nearside of the engine. The only attempt at streamlining was a leather fairing between the brief scuttle and the seats, and an undershield beneath the engine. *The Autocar* mentions provision for water-cooling of the back tyres from a tank on the car. The Fiat was said to develop 175 hp, against 130 hp of the 16.2-litre GP Fiats, and weighed 1 ton 9 cwt. 66 lb. Nazzaro, unlike Newton, carried a riding mechanic.

It might have been thought that Sir George Abercromby — who drove a smaller 58 hp Fiat at the Track (his colours were navy-blue coat and sleeves, red cap) — would have been delighted with 'Mephistopheles', which beat Edge's six-cylinder shaft-drive Napier, and the loudly acclaimed 120 mph lap. Not a bit of it! He made it known soon after the Match Race that he did not intend to take over the car, on which he seems to have paid a deposit of over £800, and he did not enter it for the Montagu Cup Race for which he had specifically ordered it. This put Mr D'Arcy Baker, Manager of Fiat in this country, in something of a predicament. He had placed the order for 'Mephistopheles' and stood by it when Turin insisted that they must make two identical cars. There was less demand for racing cars in 1908 than when Brooklands had opened, he argued, and the Fiat Company would be lucky to sell the car for £1,000. There had been the expense of bringing Nazzaro and his mechanics over to Long Acre to tune up the car, the engine of which had had to be completely stripped on the eve of the Match Race. D'Arcy Baker felt he had no option but to sue.

Another giant Fiat of the early period.

The case was heard before Mr Justice Darling at the end of the year, and the big Fiat meanwhile languished under a dust-sheet. Whether doubt over the timing influenced Sir George I don't know, but certainly he disliked the idea of Fiat having a second car identical to his own, which, if Nazzaro chose to drive it, could easily beat an amateur driver.

A settlement was reached whereby Sir George accepted the Fiat for £1,250, both parties paying their own costs and withdrawing all insinuations, and in 1910 he appeared at Brooklands with 'Mephistopheles', the car looking just as it did when Nazzaro drove it, even to the leather side valances. During 1909 this Guards officer had raced 8.9 hp Sizaire-Naudin, 36 hp Crossley and 40 hp Napier cars at the Track, but in the 1910 May Handicap he was on the scratch mark in 'Mephistopheles' and did his first flying lap at 106.38 mph. The second lap was completed at 101.59 mph, and then the big Fiat retired. This speed is significant in view of the fact that the old car was proclaimed by Fiat to be in excellent condition after Nazzaro's race, and now, on its reappearance, it lapped very close to its best hand-timed speed of 1908. It ran in a sprint race and was out again, still on scratch, at the Midsummer Meeting, when interest centred round the Fiat, in which it allowed any other entrant 62 seconds start. Its lap speed was beaten by Stirling's 60 hp Brasier (102.22 mph) and by Wildegose in the 60 hp Itala later owned by Cecil Clutton (101.80 mph), so Sir George was probably displeased. In subsequent races he ran his Napier, before returning to Scotland for the shooting. It seems likely that Sir George had initiated this last race in the hope of ridding himself of a liability.

In 1911 Mrs Macklin was billed to attack the world half-mile record at Brooklands with the old Fiat but it only managed 90.94 mph. Otherwise,

Nazzaro and the Fiat 'Mephistopheles' which won the Match Race against the Napier 'Samson' at Brooklands in 1908, and was electrically-timed to lap at 121.64 mph, queried in some quarters ever since. Never mind! Most of the ladies fell for the famous Italian driver.

The Fiat
'Mephistopheles' as
Capt. John Duff found
it in a Fulham Mews
garage after the First
World War, and
purchased for £100.

for two years 'Mephistopheles', and indeed Fiats of any sort, were absent from Brooklands, but at the 1913 Whitsun Meeting C. R. Engley appeared with the car which had achieved so much acclaim in Nazzaro's hands half-a-dozen years earlier. At least, everything points to this car being 'Mephistopheles', although, as stated earlier, the engine dimensions declared come out to 20.9 litres. It appears that Sir George had been posted abroad, and had returned his Napier to S. F. Edge, selling the Fiat to Noel Macklin (later of Invicta and Railton fame), who presumably sold it to Engley. Early in trouble in the 10th 100 mph Long Handicap, from the scratch mark, after the car had been pushed ignominiously to get it going, Engley non-started in both his races at the Midsummer Meeting, but managed a lap at 93.09 mph on August Bank Holiday, and laps of 98.43 and 98.62 mph at the Autumn Meeting. During the abbreviated 1914 season there was no further sign of the big Fiat. (Incidentally, attempting to identify Engley's Fiat brought up a typical instance of the pitfalls a motoring historian has to face. *The Autocar* at the time remarked first of all that they believed it had 'the same dimensions as the Fiat driven by Nazzaro himself' — they were making the point that it was the largest engine ever seen at Brooklands, with the exception of the A. Lee Guinness Darracq. Even at the 'inflated' size of 20,981 cc this was incorrect; Hemery's 1911 Benz was of 21,504 cc. In a later issue the car is quite definitely described as the 1907 Nazzaro car, but earlier it was described as the Fiat 'whose previous owners were Sir George Abercromby, Baker White, and Noel Macklin'. Baker White seems to have had the second of these Fiats, while if Macklin also owned 'Mephistopheles', the Fiat he actually raced at Brooklands for Paul Mayer was a 1906 or 1907 GP car. Just to make matters more difficult, Sir George Abercromby told me he thought Macklin put the engine into a boat, but perhaps it was Macklin's GP Fiat that suffered that fate.

After the interlude for war, John Duff, later to make his name with 3-

litre Bentleys, discovered 'Mephistopheles' in a Fulham mews-garage. At the time he was racing an S61 Fiat at Brooklands, but it was getting rather long in the tooth so, encouraged by Major R. F. Cooper, who was a friend of Count Zborowski, he bought 'Mephistopheles' (it is said for £100) and proceeded to get it into trim. It still retained its wooden wheels, but Duff gave it a radiator cowl and streamlined tail, and a body with a proper scuttle, while I think a different, rounded-top radiator was fitted, and a revised exhaust system with tail-pipe was made up. The old car was repainted black, with a white body. Unfortunately, when I interviewed Duff at his racehorse training establishment near Newmarket, some years before his fatal riding accident, he did not remember details.

Duff and Cooper shared the entry of the Fiat at the 1921 Whitsun Meeting, where it was handicapped to lap at 102.69 mph but failed to start. Duff also non-started in the big car's first race at the next meeting, but in the '100 Long' did a standing lap at 89.78 mph and flying laps at 106.88 and 100.82 mph, although was unplaced from scratch. At the August Meeting the Fiat finished second to the 1912 Lorraine-Dietrich in the 'Lightning Short', with a standing-start lap at 91.52 mph and a flying lap at 108.27 mph, but after a standing-start lap at 91.17 mph retired from the 'Long' when the pistons cracked and damaged the engine.

Duff did not run the big Fiat again that year but, having sold his smaller Fiat, concentrated on 'Mephistopheles' during 1922, Harry Ricardo installing light-alloy pistons in an endeavour to increase engine speed, while wire wheels were now fitted. The car was ready by the Whitsun Meeting of 1922 and lapped at 89.78 and 107.10 mph in the 'Lightning Short', being caught by Zborowski's 'Chitty-Bang-Bang'. In the '100 Short' the Fiat finished 3rd (lap speeds: 90.63 and 109.46 mph) with only the

The end of 'Mephistopheles'? Its engine 'blew-up' in sensational fashion in 1922 when John Duff was racing it. But Ernest Eldridge gave it a new lease of life, and took the Land Speed Record in 1924, by installing an even larger Fiat aero engine.

Viper lapping faster, and that car was slower away. However, Duff retired sensationally in the 'Lightning Long', before completing a lap, when the new pistons proved too much for the old cylinder blocks and aged crankcase (about which Ricardo had warned Duff) and the rear pair came out through the bonnet, hung over the heads of Duff and L. G. Callingham of Shell, his passenger, then crashed back into place, showering the occupants with metal debris! Duff managed to pull up safely, but it seemed as if 'Mephistopheles' would henceforth be merely a motor-racing legend.

On the contrary, the car went on to achieve even greater fame, E. A. D. Eldridge taking over the famous car and installing in its chassis a 300 hp six-cylinder Fiat aviation engine as described in my *Aero-Engined Racing Cars at Brooklands* (Foulis/Haynes, 1992).

4. The 1908 Grand Prix Napiers

For the 1908 French Grand Prix, the Napier Company of Acton, London, built a team of cars with lattice side-members to their chassis, double cantilever back springs and six-cylinder inlet-over-exhaust engines of 126.2×152.4 mm or 4.97 in. × 6 in. (11,371 cc). They were also equipped, for rapid work in the pits, with detachable wire wheels. Of the latter, the Automobile Club de France would have no part and the cars were not permitted to compete. (For the same reason the 1908 Grand Prix Italas ran with fixed wooden wheels in the French Grand Prix, although detachable rims were allowed; it wasn't until its Brooklands appearance in 1910 that the Itala, owned by Cecil Clutton from the 1930s, was endowed with detachable wire wheels.)

Deprived of their appearance in the Grand Prix, one of the cars was taken to Brooklands, where at the 1908 August Meeting, driven by J. G. Reynolds, it took part in the 100-mile O'Gorman Trophy Race until the off-side back tyre burst and the Napier left the track as it slowed down, both Reynolds and his mechanic being thrown clear on to the grass as the car overturned. In 1909 A. Baker White, who had a stable of different horse-power cars which he raced enthusiastically at the Track — including the giant Fiat which Felice Nazzaro drove there that year — owned another Grand Prix Napier, or it may have been the same one. It retired from the August Senior Handicap because of a distributor lead coming adrift, but it had run in the Grand Prix Sweepstakes, when it lapped at 82.42 mph.

Astley also obtained one of the Grand Prix Napiers. There was an amusing occasion when Astley took Baron de Zuylen de Nyevelt de Haar, President of the ACF and a Committee member of the BARC, for some laps on this green Napier, the elderly gentleman having refused the Locke Kings' offer of a ride round inside a limousine. Lent a dirty old dust coat and pulling his cap well down, this august gentlemen was driven at up to some 100 mph, and proved himself a thorough sportsman. Astley sold the car back to the Napier Company, after he had had an easy win with it in that year's 'Grand Prix' race at the Track, to concentrate on the aeroplane he was building at Brooklands in 1909.

As the Napier Company was soon to give up participation in racing these advanced team cars vanished from the competition scene. Two were given two-seater bodies and used for touring. By 1909 or 1910 the Regent Carriage Company had done such a conversion, and it is believed that an American purchaser took that Napier to the USA.

Another went to an owner in Northumberland after a utility body had been made for it, to replace the two bucket seats and large cylindrical petrol tank the car wore when found early in 1911. This intended-to-be-

temporary body was never removed, as it was found to be very useful. A large Polyrohe carburettor was fitted and, with a top-gear ratio of 1.78 to 1, the consumption of pure benzole was improved to just over 16 mpg.

It is thought that four of these Napiers had been built for the Grand Prix. The above accounts for two, and another was thought to have been burnt out. Around 1912/13 the owner of the car just described used to see a sister car in the Paddock at Brooklands.

Although it was a considerable time before the Vintage Sports-Car Club 'discovered' the delights of resuscitating such of the old giant cars as remained, those who already had a liking for aged vehicles must have been gratified when, without warning, J. S. Spencer produced one of the 1908 GP Napiers, now having the fascinating patina of age, at the 1925 Brooklands Whitsun Meeting. It may well have been the one used by the gentleman in Northumberland. It had a grey two-seater body and the wheelbase would have been 9 ft. 8 in., and the weight around 21¾ cwt. Spencer tried it out at the 1925 BARC Whitsun Meeting, in the 45th 100 mph Short Handicap race, for which he was the limit starter, on 39 seconds. Dr Benjafield, the next to be flagged away, in his 3-litre Bentley, 20 seconds later, soon caught the old GP car, which failed to complete a lap. However, things improved in the equivalent Long Handicap, in which Spencer, flagged away 17 seconds after a bunch consisting of two fast 12/50 Alvises and Capt. Waite's equally effective Austin Seven, after a slow first lap at 56.85 mph, speeded up to 73.35 mph, then to retire. Understandably, it was the slowest competitor in the race.

After missing the Brooklands Summer races, Spencer, who also raced a Brooklands Super Sports GE Austin Seven, entered his old motor-car for the August Bank Holiday Meeting. It was quickly overhauled by Turner's orange Austro-Daimler in the '100 Short', the Napier's lap speeds being 67.30 and 78.43 mph, with a start of 10 seconds on Turner. Trouble then

J. G. Reynolds with one of the 1908 Grand Prix Napiers he raced at the Track around 1909/10. Note the lattice side-members and double cantilever back springs.

*Ancient warrior! J. S.
Spencer appeared with
this 1908 GP Napier
(No. 10) at Brooklands
in 1925. The car in the
foreground is A. V.
Jackson's 12/50 Alvis,
and E. C. Gordon
England's 200-Mile
Race Austin 7 is on the
Napier's right.*

struck again in the '100 Long', after a poor standing-start lap at 56.85 mph
and a quicker one at 73.35 mph, ending in another retirement. However,
perseverance often pays, and at the Autumn Meeting the ancient Napier
performed much better, having been tuned up by none other than the
great Austin Seven exponent E. C. Gordon England, who had no doubt
supplied Spencer's other racing car. Admittedly it non-started in the '75
Short', in which the aforesaid Austro-Daimler and an Alvis dead-heated,
but in the '75 Long' it more or less came together. The Napier was handicapped to start from the 46 second mark, in a group behind an Amilcar
and an old Wolseley Moth, and leading after two laps it finished third,
beaten only by such well-known cars as a Thomas Special and the Austro-
Daimler. The laps were timed at 71.95, 82.04 and 80.33 mph, the race-aver-
age nearly 80 mph, which should have pleased the owner-driver. He was
sufficiently encouraged to enter the Napier for the '75 Long' at the 1926
Easter Meeting (its engine-size wrongly quoted in the race card) probably
preferring this to the '75 Short' handicap. After which this Napier vanished as quietly as it had appeared, never to be seen again.

I was never able to trace the Spencer family to learn more about it, but
for many years a 1908 GP engine adorned the foyer of Napier's Acton
premises, possibly from Spencer's car.

5. The 1908 Grand Prix Itala

For the 1908 French Grand Prix at Dieppe the Itala Motor Company of Turin, which also had a depot at Weybridge close to Brooklands Track, prepared a team of cars, as they had for the first of these races in 1906. The Italas, for this very important race, had four-cylinder 155×160 mm (12,076 cc) engines with low-tension ignition and overhead inlet valves, developing 100 bhp at 1,600 rpm. Final drive was by shaft, and the unladen weight was 27.8 cwt, increased in racing trim on the starting line to 32.3 cwt. The drivers in the Grand Prix were Cagno, Fournier and Piacenza. On the first lap of this 477-mile contest Lautenschlager won for Mercedes, at 69.0 mph. Cagno finished in 11th place, having averaged 58.7 mph, and Fournier was 20th, at 54.3 mph, the other car having retired with gearbox trouble.

After the race, two of these Itala cars came to Brooklands, as did other ex-Grand Prix cars — and, of course, the Locke Kings, creators of the Track, were great exponents of the make. They were raced by Eric Loder and Robert Wildegose (the latter being Works Manager of the British Itala Company). Wildegose entered by the car's owner (the brewer H. T. L. Young) lapped at 93.22 mph in the 1909 October Senior Handicap. This

The 1908 Grand Prix Itala in the form in which Robert Wildegose lapped Brooklands at 101.80 mph at the 1910 Summer BARC Meeting. Note the long starting-handle shaft, necessitated by the crude radiator cowl; such cowls were fitted not only to improve streamlining but to direct more air over a car's radiator.

car ran again in 1910 at the Summer BARC Meeting in the Brooklands All-Comers' Plate of 100 sovs, and won. It did all six flying laps at over 100 mph, its best at 101.80 mph, fitted with disc wheels and a cowled radiator. (Mr Wildegose was present at the dinner, arranged in December 1946 by Cecil Clutton, Anthony Heal and Laurence Pomeroy, to celebrate the re-publication of Gerald Rose's book *A Record of Motor Racing* with the author — Clutton then owning the Itala.) The same combination was out again for one more appearance at Brooklands, in 1911, but after coming home a poor third in the March Sprint Race the great car was given a touring body by Vincent's of Reading, and Rudge wire wheels in place of the wooden-spoked wheels, which had sufficed for the Grand Prix, and was used for touring and by Dunlop after the war for tyre testing.

I am delighted to be able to recount the subsequent life of this 1908 Itala, because it has been quite outstanding. Having survived the 1914/18 war, it was driven in 1920 from London up to Diss in Norfolk and given to the landlord of the Scole Inn by a friend of his. It was put in a shed behind the public house, where in 1927 John S. Pole (who was later to own the ex-Count Zborowski White Mercedes and run it in the 1929 BRDC 500 Mile Race — see *Aero-Engined Racing Cars at Brooklands*, Foulis/Haynes, 1992) stopped to have lunch. He happened to go round to the back of the Inn, and saw in the shed this huge old touring car, covered in crates, bottles, chicken manure, weeds — the lot. In 1936, when the VSCC was starting its quest for really big racing cars to compete in its events, Pole, who had left the RAF in 1932, went back to Diss one Sunday and, sure enough, the old Itala was still occupying the same shed, more dirty and forlorn than ever. He purchased it for £25. A week later he returned with two friends and a 30-cwt Morris truck, and within three days they had got the ancient warrior running, at the expense of the Morris's gearbox. When the Itala fired-up while on tow, it thrust the luckless vehicle roughly out of its way before Pole could get the clutch out, and sprung the chassis of the truck so much that the bottom of the gearbox fell out. With dust and cobwebs

The Itala photographed around 1912, with the Vincents' touring body it had by then acquired. Standing by it is W. C. Harris, who used to help Robert Wildegose work on this and a 45 hp Itala from 1911 to 1914 when the owner, H. L. T. Young, lived at Lambourn House, Berkshire. Mr Harris was united with the old Itala in later years and attended its birthday party which Sam Clutton gave at Silverstone, when Harris was 82.

blowing over him, Pole kept the 12 litres of engine running, and drove triumphantly back into the shed.

The next morning about 20 people from the Inn — chef, waiters, maids and anyone else who could cling on to the car — were given a run up the road at some 70 mph. Pole had had to renew the wiring and cut the tyres off the rims, but he got the Itala running properly and used it for some appropriate events; for instance, winning the Edwardian class at the second VSCC speed trials in May 1936, at Aston Clinton. The impression the car made on those of my generation was profound, for never had we seen monster racing cars from the pre-war age in action. Seeking such a car Cecil ('Sam') Clutton, CBE, a prominent member of the VSCC, took over the Itala from Pole, and at the next VSCC speed trials, this time at Bramshill, he also made best Edwardian time with it, in 25.9 seconds, and he won the class on the handicap system he had himself devised to suit such cars, and which the VSCC still uses. At the May 1938 Shelsley-Walsh hill-climb at the historic hill near Worcester, Clutton gave the ordinary spectators a chance to see for the first time a big Edwardian in action, and the Itala caused quite a stir.

From then on, Clutton drove his mighty car in trials, more speed-trials, and in speed hill-climbs, as well as racing it. For a time, Peter Robertson-Rodger was a co-owner. Gearbox maladies intervened in 1938, but in 1939 Sam won a three-lap race for such cars at the Crystal Palace circuit, beating Anthony Heal's S61 Fiat (see Chapter 11) and Dick Nash's 1912 GP Lorraine-Dietrich (see Chapter 10), the only cars of similar pace. Indeed, the Fiat may have been somewhat quicker on a good day, and the Lorraine likewise when it was running properly. At that time no rev-counter was fitted, and Sam used to go on until no more speed was possible in the gear in use. Afterwards a rev-counter kept him to 1,650 rpm. Just before Brooklands Track was closed to ordinary mortals in 1940

The old Itala turned up again in the 1930s and was acquired by Cecil ('Sam') Clutton, whose campaigning of it started the interest in the giant Edwardian racing cars among members of the Vintage Sports-Car Club. No wonder! For this is how the spectators saw Sam's first appearance with the 12-litre Itala at Shelsley-Walsh, with the touring bodywork made for it by Vincents of Reading before the First World War.

The massive four-cylinder engine of the GP Itala, which never foresook its low-tension ignition system. Today it is still driven at suitable events by Johnty Williamson.

Clutton took the Itala there, when it was timed at 20 seconds for the standing-start ¹/₄-mile and at 85 mph over the ¹/₂-mile.

After the war, Clutton continued to use the Itala regularly, and even took it to Dieppe on its 40th birthday, where in 1908 it had run in the French Grand Prix. Indeed, the quite remarkable thing is that he continued to compete with it for a span of more than 50 years, until his demise in 1991 at the age of 81 — an unique achievement, especially as he owned many other vintage cars and used these very frequently as well. To list all the Itala's successes when driven by Sam or its co-owners Jack and Johnty' Williamson would fill a lot of space. Let me just say that in 1947 Mr Wildegose presented the Vintage Sports-Car Club with the Itala Trophy, in appreciation of the performances put up by Clutton in the car he once raced, and this is competed for regularly at the Club's Itala Trophy race meetings. In some events thereafter Dr Bob Ewen drove the car, experiencing a leaking radiator and the foot brake on fire in the racing at Gransden later in 1947; but in 1950 all was well again, and he climbed Prescott in 57.16 seconds. In the 1952 Pomeroy Trophy contest, the Itala gave 16.7 mpg of petrol and lapped Silverstone Club circuit at 64.56 mph, with Ewen up. Later he set a Prescott time of 55.89 seconds.

The first VSCC Anglo-American Rally in 1954 saw the old motor car run a bearing, but it had recovered for the VSCC's 21st birthday party at Goodwood in 1955, when Jack Williamson's distinguished passengers in the Itala were motoring historian Baron Petiet and Charles Jarrott's one-time racing mechanic Cecil Bianchi. Bob Ewen died in 1961, so Sam went back to maintaining and driving the Itala for years hence, and Johnty Williamson continues to compete with it from time to time, intriguing most of those who see and hear its thunderous take-off.

Memories of Sam sitting high in his seat and flinging this splendid motor car about like a modern racing car remain with me. One of Cecil Clutton's ambitions was to climb Prescott with the Itala in under 55 seconds. I cannot resist including his own account of how he accomplished

this, at the Bugatti Owners' Club hill-climb course near Cheltenham:

Cecil Clutton in the 1908 Itala, appropriately in the veteran car class, leaving the start-line at Lewes, near Eastbourne, at the Bugatti Owners' Club speed trials in August 1936.

I had never succeeded in doing this in over 10 years of concentrated effort, so that by 1962, with the combined age of car and driver already totalling 105, it began to look as though we never really should. So when, on August 19th, the course was perfect and the car on top of its form, I decided it was then, if ever. Clutch in at 800 rpm, bash through to second just past the commentator's hut, under the bridge and start braking just past the apple tree. Toe and heel into bottom for the orchard and to hell with the rev-counter up to Pardon (nearly 2,000 rpm, but don't tell Jack). Check spin, back into 2nd, pump up pressure; resist temptation to brake until well past the half-way hut, and give a sharp twitch on the steering wheel to bring the back round and break away the front wheels. With luck this sets the car up to go through the esses in one continuous sweep without any broadsides or corrections. Then up to the semi-circle, slow to 1,200 rpm (30 mph; sure I could do this a bit faster if I were braver) and 1,650 over the finish line, still in 2nd. And it was 54.85 seconds, my ambition achieved and a new Edwardian record.'

The Vintage Sports-Car Club has used the same short course ever since, and at the time of writing the Edwardian record stands at 52.04 seconds, established in 1980 to the credit of Nigel Arnold-Forster driving his 5-litre 1913 Bugatti.

6. The Blitzen-type Benz

The impressive 1909 Blitzen Benz, which in America was named the 'Lightning Benz' and which, in 1911 at Daytona, gave Burman the Land Speed Record at 141.37 mph. The record was not recognized as official in Europe, but this was probably the quickest of these very fast cars.

The Blitzen Benz was the popular name given to a large car which the Benz Company brought out in 1909. It had been designed by Hans Nibel and was like the 150 hp racing Benz (the engine of which, it may be remembered, was identical to that in the 1912 Grand Prix Lorraine-Dietrich cars) except for forced-feed lubrication and a bore and stroke of 185×200 mm, giving a capacity of 21,504 cc. The RAC rating of this huge four-cylinder engine was no less than 84.8 hp. The final drive was by side chains, the sprocket size being in the region of 44/44, and the wheelbase of the racing version is quoted by David Scott-Moncrieff, in *Three Pointed Star*, as 8 ft. 6 in. Other authorities speak of a wheelbase of about 9 ft. 4 in. This same authority says that the great car was at first called by its maker the 100 hp model, later the 200 hp. However, so far as

the English market was concerned, it appears that the 100 hp Benz was the 130×190 mm car, and that it was not until 1913 that the 200 hp car was available here, presumably in longer wheelbase form than the, by now, very famous racing versions.

The first appearance of a Blitzen Benz in England was at Brooklands on 8 November 1909, when Victor Hemery used one to break world records. The big Benz was entered by Cullum and Niven-Jock. Hemery first went for standing-start records, being timed over the ¹/₂-mile at 70.406 mph, over the kilometre at 71.409 mph, and over the mile at 87.233 mph. The Benz was then set to lap Brooklands as fast as possible. Hemery covered the ¹/₂-mile at 127.877 mph, the kilometre at 125.947 mph and the mile at 115.923 mph, the mile being slower than the other runs because Hemery had difficulty in taking the banking. His kilometre run ranked as the World Land Speed Record.

Nothing more was heard in England of these gigantic Benz cars until a Blitzen Benz arrived for L. G. ('Cupid') Hornsted to drive. It arrived here just prior to the 1913 Motor Show, and Hornsted lost little time in attacking records with it at Brooklands. After it had been fitted with Palmer cord tyres, Hornsted broke the world standing-start ¹/₂-mile and kilometre records with it on 22 December 1913, at 70.47 and 73.47 mph, respectively.

Before the car arrived in this country, Hornsted had been to the Benz factory and specified valves with normal seats instead of the Benz triple-seated valves, and struts between piston crowns and gudgeon-pins. The car was said to be geared to give 140 mph at 1,400 rpm, using 44/44 sprockets.

Hornsted's ultimate aim was the world hour record, held by Goux (Peugeot) at 106.22 mph, but the available tyres defeated him. On 14 January 1914, however, he broke the world 2-mile record at 122.05 mph, the 5-mile record at 116.08 mph and Class J records for the ¹/₂-mile and mile at 123.83 and 123.54 mph, respectively. Later that month Hornsted added the world standing-start mile record at 87.34 mph and the Class J 10-mile record at 112.57 mph to his bag.

In longer assaults, hoping for the hour record, the Benz developed a tendency for steam pockets to form between the inlet valves of cylinders 1 and 2, and 3 and 4, so the block was drilled to take ³/₄ in. gas adapters, and copper pipes led to the radiator. But always the tyres proved the limiting factor, their life on the back wheels never exceeding 60 miles. On one occasion Hornsted experienced a record skid when a cover disintegrated and locked a back wheel. *The Car* described the incident as follows:

Mr L. G. Hornsted, the famous racing motorist, had what he called an exciting experience recently. It was at Brooklands, of course, and it happened with the big 200 hp Benz. Hornsted took her out for a trial spin to get an approximate idea of what she really could do in an hour, and from a standing start did the first five laps at an average speed of 111.89 mph. Feeling comfortable, and knowing that the car was running well, he began to let her out a bit, and did the sixth lap in 83 secs, which is, roughly, 121 mph. By the time he came off the big banking on to the railway straight the car was travelling at over 130 mph. Halfway down the railway straight the off hind wheel struck a biggish stone with a particularly malicious knife edge and the bump practically cut the tyre in half transversely. The result of this was that a strip of the tread fouled the driving chain and the car slewed round, and travelled some 60 or 80 yds, practically broadside on. She then turned completely round twice, and as she was half-way through the third turn she struck the banking.

Capt. Toop, who used to accompany Hornsted in the Blitzen Benz, wearing a face mask against the January cold, before lapping the Track in 1914.

This stopped her turning, and she began to run up the banking tail first. In a flash Hornsted realised that the banking was not steep enough to stop her wild career, and as a last resort he changed down to third, accelerated violently, and banged his clutch in just in time. The huge car hesitated, and then came slithering and sliding down again, to be eventually brought to a standstill some way farther along, with her nearside wheels over the inside edge of the track. The Rudge-Whitworth wheels had stood the terrible strain in a wonderful manner, and both Hornsted and Toop (who was acting as mechanic) were unscratched.

Two of these 21½-litre monsters were still racing at the track in 1922. One of them was entered by J. L. Dunne of the British Benz Company, of Grafton Street, for H. V. Barlow to drive, and the other was entered in the name of Major R. F. Cooper (who was undeterred by the death of his brother, who had been killed testing his V8 Cooper Clerget the year before) for his friend Count Zborowski to drive. Both were genuine 185×200 mm Blitzen cars, and both were painted white, the German racing colour.

Barlow's Benz was announced, no doubt by some forerunner of today's publicity agents, as the 'new hush hush post-war Benz'. In fact, as I shall show, there is good reason to suppose that it was none other than Hornsted's pre-war car, with the radiator cowl removed to reveal the impressive snout-nosed Blitzen radiator. It ran on Continental tyres, from which company Barlow no doubt received a bonus.

The Zborowski Benz was referred to by *The Autocar* as the car which had done 147 mph at Daytona in 1911, but was unquestionably, to my mind, Hemery's old Benz of 1909. It had what looks like a 'pirate' radiator, no doubt found amongst Zborowski's stock of old car parts, and at first had a small fuel tank set in line with the chassis and exposed behind the seats. Before it was raced, however, a long streamlined tail was added, I think by Bligh Bros of Canterbury, where the Count had his bodies made. I suspect that because of ill-feeling over the war the Benz Company

After the Armistice, Count Louis Zborowski drove one of the big Benz cars at Brooklands until he decided that it was too dangerous even for him to tame. It is seen here (right) at the garages above the Brooklands entrance road, in company with his straight-eight Ballot.

A close-up view of the Zborowski Benz, the tail of which was made by Bligh Bros. of Canterbury. By 1920 the car was getting a bit ancient, having been brought to Brooklands by Victor Hemery in 1909, where it raised the LSR officially to 125.95 mph that November.

had not liked to enter the Barlow car in 1921, while Zborowski was too busy that year evolving his two 'Chittys'.

In any event, Zborowski appeared in Major Cooper's Benz at the 1922 BARC Easter meeting, in the 100 mph Short Handicap. Starting from the 22 sec. mark, the old car made by far the best time (88.1 mph) to the Fork, apart from Segrave's 5-litre Sunbeam, and finished second to that car after lapping at 99.61 mph. This earned a re-handicap of six seconds in the 100 mph Long Handicap, but Zborowski averaged 90.63 mph to the Fork, a speed bettered only by the Sunbeam and, lapping at 106.88 and 104.85 mph in this difficult and dangerous car, he won at 99.84 mph.

Thus encouraged to risk his life again, Zborowski ran the Benz at the Summer Meeting. He found himself on scratch in the Private Competitors' Handicap, and although he arrived back at the Fork at 92.06 mph, and lapped at 104.63 mph, he could not do better than a poor fourth. Nor was the big car placed in the '100 Short', for after doing 82.1 mph to the Fork, Zborowski retired, and the car failed to start in the '100 Long'.

Neither Benz was entered for the Whitsun Meeting in July, but later that month Barlow's car caused a sensation at the Essex MC Brooklands meeting. It left the paddock for the start on fire. This was extinguished, but the big white car began to emit a long trail of black smoke and finally burst into flames — the driver and D.S. Gowing of Bradestone Hall, Norwich* , his overalls alight, hastily abandoning their seats. They were covered in soot but not seriously hurt. Press reports declared the car to be almost totally destroyed, but a Brooklands official had brought the fire under control, and both Benz were in the Race Card for the BARC August Bank Holiday meeting.

Perhaps Barlow's misfortune had given him a lenient handicap. In any event, the Benz got away from the 8 sec. mark in a field of five in the Lightning Short Handicap and won at 105 mph, after lapping at 97.8 and

*But see page 55.

113.97 mph. It should have met Major Cooper's Benz in the '100 Short' but Zborowski non-started. The other Benz, described as bumping along the top of the bankings in its previous race, and looking hard to hold, was now re-handicapped to 'owes 10 sec.' (which would have given

The brave Count Zborowski, whose aero-engined 'Chitty-Bang-Bangs' became a legend, at speed in the Benz on the Brooklands banking. Its best lap was at 106.88 mph.

A crowd of Brooklands admirers surround Zborowski's Benz.

Zborowski 14 sec. start). In spite of laps at 96.77 and 113.19 mph, Barlow was unplaced, and an unfortunate fatal accident involving Gibson's Vauxhall resulted in the remainder of the meeting being cancelled.

In the meantime, Barlow had written so lurid an account of driving the Benz for the *Daily Mail* that he found Brooklands habitués pulling his leg unmercifully.

Zborowksi found his old Benz insufficiently fast and withdrew it from the Essex MC Championship meeting, but J. L. Dunne entered the other Benz for the final Brooklands meeting of 1923. Capt. John Duff was to drive it in place of Horace Barlow. He got the large and ancient automobile going really fast in the 100 mph Short Handicap, after failing to complete a lap in the 'Lightning Short' because of tyre trouble. From scratch he lapped at 98.2 and 114.49 mph, and came up the finishing straight at about 120 mph. This proved too much for the brakes, even though the 'lightning finishing line' was in use. Duff pulled the speed down considerably but could not take the turn and went over the top of the banking. Neither Duff nor his passenger were unduly damaged, but the Benz, which had cut down a telegraph pole in its flight, was somewhat battered about, and Clement was called upon to drive the Bentley to victory in the next race in place of Duff.

Barlow used this episode to slang all and sundry, and received a severe rating in the correspondence pages of the motor papers, including a dressing down from Parry Thomas. But, as a historian, I am grateful for these acrimonious letters, because Hornsted was drawn into the fray and the wording of his comments implies clearly that, at this date at any rate, he was aware that the car Barlow and Duff had resuscitated *was* his old Blitzen Benz.

The correspondence that appeared in *The Motor* following Capt. Duff's accident was as follows:

Count Louis Zborowski in the Paddock at Brooklands with the aged 200 hp Benz before the streamlined tail and bonnet sides had been added. Note the longitudinally-mounted petrol tank.

Captain Duff's Accident.

Re Capt. Duff's accident at the last Brookland's meeting, numerous
people have asked me if I can give any explanation of the cause. As I
have driven the car for several months, it may interest your readers to
know that my explanation is that I do not think Duff was fit. He had
taken out of himself an enormous amount of energy when he broke the
double 12-hour record on the Bentley, a stupendous feat to accomplish
single-handed. There are limits to the endurance of the human frame,
and it was quite apparent to me on the Thursday and Friday, while
practising, that he was extremely tired and over-anxious. The car on the
day before the race was giving him a lot of trouble, and only those who
have prepared cars for a race know the anxiety and worry involved.
While watching his last practice laps on Friday evening, it did not seem
to me that he was driving well, and to drive the Benz it is absolutely
necessary to be fit, as a couple of laps on that car takes more out of the
driver than in an ordinary racing car for 20 laps. It is impossible to give
anyone who has not sat in the car any idea of the enormous strain and
concentration and brute strength required to hold this car on the banking. The car went past the grand-stand, in the finish of the race, at a ter-
rific speed, quite 115 miles per hour, and to me it seemed certain that
the throttle was still open, and I was hoping that he would not endeavour to stop, but take her up the banking and as high as possible and
carry on down the straight, finishing another lap, as I had to do on
August Bank Holiday. It was no question of brakes. If it had been possible for him to have reversed the engine, it would have made no difference at the speed he was travelling. The only way to stop the Benz, in a
short distance, is, when the car crosses the line, to tip the gear lever into
neutral, turn the petrol tap off under the steering wheel (no easy feat at
that speed), and apply the foot brakes and hand brake alternately every
fifth of a second to prevent them seizing up. When I tried the car on
Thursday, the brakes were good and very powerful, but brakes are really of little use at 120 miles per hour. Another reason possibly was that
the enormous suction of this engine may have caused the throttle to
stick open, and if this happened it would be absolutely impossible for
him to do anything. Switching off the engine would have only made
matters worse, as the car is unbalanced and unsteerable when running
against compression.

If cars keep on improving in speed next season as they have done
this, the finish for the big cars will have to take place at the fork, otherwise we shall see more go over the top. Several small cars during the
last two or three meetings have experienced difficulty in pulling up,
and braking a car at high speeds will always be dangerous, owing to
the brakes being liable to seize and lock the wheels.

Visitors to Brooklands must not blame Duff, as the odds against
pulling up were heavily against him, and it might have happened to
anybody at the speed he crossed the finishing line.

Capt. Auger, who acted as his mechanic, and who went round with
me at every meeting in which the car has run, deserves some recogni-
tion for his pluck in going as passenger in every practice lap and meeting in which the car has run. Brookland's habitués will no doubt
remember that he was in the car when I was driving, and we looked

over the banking at 120 miles per hour at the previous meeting. After that experience, to continue to go round in the car as a passenger with a strange driver shows courage possessed by few.

HORACE BARLOW.

Mr J. G. P. Thomas on the Benz Accident.

I notice in a recent issue of your paper that Mr. Barlow has attempted to explain the accident to Capt. Duff's car by more or less suggesting that it was caused by faulty judgment on the part of Capt. Duff.

As I happened to be running in the same race, and was, as a matter of fact, within 30 yards of Capt. Duff's car during the whole of the race, and was within five yards of him when he went over the top, I am perhaps in a position to correct the impression which Mr. Barlow has tried to create.

In the first case, Capt. Duff was driving the Benz at a far higher speed than it had ever previously been driven in a race at Brooklands. I believe I am correct in stating that the maximum lap speed ever previously obtained by the Benz was about 112 miles per hour.

I notice that the Benz concern have been advertising a lap speed of 114 miles per hour, but as I was behind the car during this particular race, and was actually gaining on him the whole of the second lap, and my own speed was only 112 miles per hour, it is obvious that some error in calculation must have been made.

Since that actual race my own speed in the Leyland has been increased by approximately five miles per hour, and my car was timed to lap at 117 on the particular day when Capt. Duff was running, and it was obvious to me that the car was travelling at a far higher speed than had ever been attained previously.

On entering the straight we were travelling at 120 miles per hour at least, and, considering the finishing line which we were then using, it was only to be expected that some difficulty would be experienced in pulling up. I myself had very great difficulty in preventing my car from following the Benz, and, as mentioned previously, I was within five yards of him when he went over the top.

I carefully examined the skid marks of the Benz and my own car on the day following the accident, which clearly showed that the Benz had actually skidded for the last 10 ft. or 12 ft. broadside on, up the track, which confirmed the opinion which I had formed while I was actually following him.

Fortunately the Leyland has a much better weight distribution so I was able to take a wider sweep at the bank, and did a considerable amount of side-skidding long before the top of the track was reached.

In conclusion, I think that great credit should be given to Capt. Duff for putting up such a good speed on such a car, and I feel sure that everyone will be pleased to hear that both he and his mechanic, who are well on the road to recovery, are already discussing the car in which they will race next year.

J. G. P. THOMAS

Mr. L. G. Hornsted's Views.

Re Mr. Horace Barlow's views on Capt. Duff's accident. I have never bothered you with my views before, but would beg you to air them for me in this case. If he will allow me to say so, I consider Capt. Duff one of the best drivers of cars on Brooklands.

Mr. H. Barlow's ideas of how to stop the Benz are entirely novel to me. I have never tipped the lever into neutral (and if in neutral, why bother with petrol tap?). The ordinary methods of stopping a car are quite good enough: Switch off, leaving gear and clutch in, shut down jet and throttle, stand on foot brake and pull hand brake, and the old Benz will stop as quickly as any four-brake car.

May I suggest that, as the Big Benz has done some of its greatest speeds with myself at the wheel, the above facts can be taken as the result of experience?

Capt. Duff's accident, I am sure, was due to no fault of his, for a cooler or better driver does not exist, and many people might learn from him rather than try to teach him.

The Benz is one of the best balanced chassis I have ever driven, and because it "sat down" so well it was always the envy of other drivers.

Be it clearly understood, I give no reason for Capt. Duff's accident; he is the only one to give the true reason, and inexpert surmises will probably make him laugh as heartily as they have me.

I cordially agree with one thing in Mr. Barlow's lengthy letter—the straight at Brooklands must not be used for cars capable of more than 90 m.p.h.

L. G. HORNSTED.
Chemnitz.

A Reply to Thomas and Hornsted.

Replying to Mr. Thomas, I did not suggest in any part of my letter that the Benz went over the top through faulty judgment of Capt. Duff. For the benefit of Mr. Thomas, I will requote: "Visitors to Brooklands must not blame Duff, as it might have happened to anybody at the speed the car travelled past the grand-stand." To requote Mr. Thomas: "In the actual race I myself had very great difficulty in preventing my car from following the Benz," and yet he had plenty of time to watch the Benz go over and see more than people on the grand-stand. Personally, I thought Mr. Thomas had his hands full with his own affairs at the time he mentions. He tries to belittle my performance on the Benz, when he received a start and ran me a very bad second; he describes how he was catching me in the last lap, and yet his time was only 112 m.p.h., and then he says that the Benz concern (meaning, I take it, the English company in Grafton Street) advertise my actual speed as 114 m.p.h. My actual speed as returned by one of the officials was 115.2 m.p.h. Now I will inform him why he thought he was catching the Benz. Capt. Auger, my mechanic, signalled for me to ease up at the end of the railway straight, and when I arrived at the Sunbeam sheds I shut off and tipped into neutral, and coasted in for the last half mile, yet lapped at 115.2 m.p.h. Mr. Thomas may have believed that his Leyland was catching the Benz (Capt. Auger can verify the above statement). No, Mr. Thomas, your Leyland is a very fast and wonderful car, but for acceleration and speed it is not mapped with the old 1910 Benz.

Now, Mr. Hornsted, your letter is really funny and surprising. You must have forgotten all about the Benz. I was taught by the German driver who brought the car over, and his first instructions to me were not to switch off until the car was in the paddock and mechanic got out and pulled half-compression mechanism into operation, otherwise the engine was liable to pre-ignite and back-fire, setting the carburetter on fire or lifting off the top of the cylinders. I was also taught immediately to turn off the petrol-jet tap, so that the engine would run on the pilot jet. A more ridiculous statement to make than that the old Benz will stop as quickly as any four-braked car (I take it Mr. Hornsted means braking four wheels?) I have never heard. If so, why did not Capt. Duff pull up? Even to compare the brakes on the Benz with the latest four-wheel brakes simply shows that Mr. Hornsted has had no experience with the system; otherwise he would not make such absurd statements.

Most readers will remember how Mr. Park stopped the 3-litre Vauxhall at Brooklands a few meetings back; when travelling at nearly 90 m.p.h. the car stopped dead in a few lengths. I would like to see Mr. Hornsted travelling in the Benz at 90 m.p.h. pull up in four times the distance.

Surely, Mr. Hornsted, there are others who are just as capable of driving the Benz as yourself. While running in a new piston the evening before the Championship Meeting my best time down the straight was 128$\frac{1}{2}$ m.p.h., which beats your best time, and the car was not all out or anything near it. Another statement you make is about the way the Benz sits on the track, the envy of all the other drivers. I will leave visitors to Brooklands to form their own opinions as to the other drivers being envious. Are they? My opinion is that if the car would only let the driver keep in the seat along the members' banking the Benz could do 150 m.p.h. or more down the railway straight. As I stated in my previous letter, various things may have happened—throttle stuck open, clutch seized, and Capt. Duff with either of these troubles would stand no chance. Everybody knows why he went over the top: he was travelling too fast to pull up in the distance from the finishing post. If the car gave trouble in any way, nobody can explain this except himself.

Mr. Thomas suggests the distribution of weight was wrong. I do not think Capt. Duff will agree with his or with Mr. L. G. Hornsted's statement that all he had to do was to stand on the foot brake and the Benz would stop.

HORACE V. BARLOW.

Mr. John F. Duff on the Brooklands Finish.

Now that a certain well-known writer of humorous fiction seems to have finished discussing my accident of October 14th, I am wondering whether you could find room in your correspondence columns for one or two observations I would like to make on the advisability of using the present finishing straight.

My own personal view is that to enter a cul-de-sac at very high speed is not desirable. I believe that my exhibition was not the first that has taken place, and, while may be perfectly safe in 99 cases out of 100, there is always the risk of the 100th case where brake failures, lost tyres, overcrowding and numerous other causes, hamper cars in reducing their speed. This trouble has not been so acutely felt in the past as it has this year, owing to the fact that cars nowadays are considerably faster than they have been. The idea of half a dozen cars crossing the line at 120 m.p.h. close together is far from attractive, those in front being afraid to brake too violently for fear of being hit in the back, and the necessity for looking round to see where all the others are, etc., all tends to increase the difficulty. With regard to the present finishing line, my experience has been that when travelling really fast there is just room, and that is all. Given any unforeseen difficulty, the risk of going over the end is quite considerable. One is tempted to ask why the finish of every race should be accompanied by very exacting strains on the brakes. Think how much more convenient to finish in the main circle of the track and simply to have to shut the throttle and coast a mile or so at the finish of a race, and come in comfortably to the paddock on the next round!

I fully realize that on a question like this it is the opinion of the majority which is all-important. It would be interesting to hear the views of one or two other drivers of the bigger and faster cars on the subject, and I have no doubt that in the event of a general opinion being expressed in one direction the Brooklands authorities might very possibly accommodate their arrangements in accordance with it.

JOHN F. DUFF.

Barlow to Duff.

Sorry I cannot let the Venerable John Duff get away with the cheap and uncalled-for gibe at my journalistic efforts on his behalf. He accuses me of writing humorous fiction; perhaps "Master John" would like some humorous facts. During the racing period at Brooklands last season "Master John" was extremely annoyed that he was not driving the Benz; so much so that he could not conceal it. Yes, John, you told everybody what you would do to "Colin Bell," if only you had the chance. Horace gave you the "chance," and no doubt you convinced several spectators at Brooklands, when you went over the top, that the Benz was not a "lady." John, you must admit the Benz is the only car that stopped you from smiling; you can take it from me I knew your thoughts as you went from the paddock. Now, "Master John," getting the funny side of humorous facts (not fiction). Do you remember telling Mr. Dunne, of the Benz Co., your racing experiences in U.S.A. before the war? Believe me, John, I can hear you now relating your experiences at Sheepshead Bay. Let us have something in print about those wonderful Yankee cars. Your description was good; like a recitation from a schoolboy of the famous V Prop.—learnt off by rote.

If I remember rightly, I can see you learning to drive in Euston Road in the year 1919. Yes, John, I can see you having your first lesson. Am I right or wrong?

Never mind, John, your performances on the big Fiat were quite good, and nobody appreciated same more than myself. You had the fastest car on the track at that time; only very few could boast a lap speed of 100 m.p.h. You made hacks of the other cars. Your performance on the Bentley will take some beating for sheer endurance. Never shall I forget the day you lapped the big Fiat at 90 m.p.h., with the main oil pipe (which had broken) tied up with your handkerchief; for real nerve this will never be equalled.

You are old enough to know that the only thing that matters and counts for anything is experience. Any driver or motorist of 10 years will tell you the first year he learnt anything about motors was after he had been driving nine years.

Have a chat with a driver of a London taxi, with the sloping bonnet, known as the "two-lunger." If you do not believe him, try to drive his taxi across London. Personally, I do not think you could do it. Yes, John, I quite agree with you—if you are lucky you will sometimes get away with it. But the funny part is that I happened to learn to drive on a "belt-driven Benz," and I have not yet got away with it.

Our learned friend Mr. Hornsted has been driving for years, John, yet he declares the Benz brakes were equal to any four-wheel brake system. You know better than that, I am quite sure.

I had almost forgotten Monsieur Thomas, of Leyland fame; he disappeared from these columns like a cat that had swallowed a "turpentine pill." I do not blame him; do you?

Why not give the readers of *The Motor* some of your pre-war motoring experiences, John; it might beat my humorous fiction.

HORACE VICTOR BARLOW.

Benz v. Leyland.

I have followed with great interest the correspondence about Mr. Duff's accident.

I have seen the Benz performing on the track many times, in the hands of both Mr. Barlow and Mr. Duff, and I cannot understand why the cause of the accident should be in doubt.

As Mr. Thomas points out, and Mr. Barlow admits, the car was entering the straight miles an hour faster than at any previous meeting, and was travelling too fast to pull up after the particular finishing line that was being used.

After all, the speed of a car like the Benz depends purely on the skill and nerve of the driver, and we cannot all expect to be equal in this respect. As it is, I think that great credit attaches to Mr. Barlow for having put up such good performances as he has.

Mr. Barlow observes that the Leyland is not "mapped" for speed and acceleration with the Benz. Considering that the Benz is a purely racing car, with an engine three times the size of the Leyland's, this is probably true. Nevertheless, given a track like Brooklands, where the personal element is such an important factor, I would confidently back Mr. Thomas on the Leyland against Mr. Barlow on the Benz over a 10-mile or longer course.

To begin with, Mr. Barlow might show his mettle by beating Mr. Thomas's 10-mile world's record—when the Benz comes back from its "overhaul."

R. D. RAILTON.

The Speed of the Benz.

In your issue of November 14th I notice a letter from a Mr. Barlow, which strikes a rather humorous note.

We are led to believe that "the old 1914 Benz" has such a magnificent engine that it is not all out at 128¹/₂ m.p.h. Then, surely to goodness, it is worth the expense of a chassis with decent brakes and able to hold the track! As for the Leyland, if Mr. Thomas can design a car of such small cubic capacity to reach a speed of 116 m.p.h., I am certain he could make a car to beat the Benz, with an increased horse-power.

I feel that most readers of *The Motor* will agree with me when I say Capt. Duff needs no teaching in race driving, after his experience with "Mephistopheles," which was a most exacting car.

W.S.N.

Captain Duff's Accident.

Are we, as readers of your most valuable paper, to be eternally persecuted by the nonsensical views of Mr. H. V. Barlow?

It is obvious, even to the most casual observer, that his desire in attacking well-known drivers such as Messrs. Hornsted, Duff, Kensington Moir, and Thomas is to achieve a certain cheap notoriety.

Possibly he has been driven to this by his lamentable failure (after years of endeavour "since the days of the belt-driven Benz") to achieve anything which would win for him the publicity so dear to his heart.

The writing of these amazing letters is unfortunately not the only form this mania for publicity has taken.

Had Messrs. Thomas and Hornsted known Mr. Barlow better they would doubtless have ignored him entirely. As it was, their letters only gave him the opportunity of once more airing his views; how ready he is to do this was shown by the lengthy article he wrote in reply to Capt. Duff's passing reference to his letters.

Why does not Mr. Barlow wait until he has achieved but a small

Another Blitzen-type Benz that enthralled the Weybridge crowds. It was driven by the flamboyant Horace Barlow, and had been driven pre-war by Hornsted.

measure of the success which has attended the efforts of even one of the gentlemen he has attacked before posing as an authority?

L. C. G. MOLLER LE CHAMPION.

Mr. Thomas to Mr. Barlow.

I shall be glad if you will find room for the following in your correspondence columns: –

Regarding Mr. Barlow's letter of December 26th, I am somewhat at a disadvantage in replying to this letter, in that I have not yet read it, having been laid up with influenza for nearly a month, but several of my friends have written to me, giving me the gist of this letter.

Apparently some explanation is required by Mr. Barlow as to why I have not replied to his various letters which have appeared in print, and I hasten to inform him that I am exceedingly busy and have not the time at my disposal which he appears to have for this class of correspondence.

J. G. P. THOMAS

Another picture of the Barlow Benz, which caught fire in one race and then took Capt. John Duff over the top of the Members' banking when he could not stop at the end of a race.

On this rather dramatic note these two white Benz vanished into limbo. Zborowski had declared his too dangerous to race, and in 1923, being concerned with Lt. Col. Clive Gallop in the construction of his Higham Special, he broke the car up in order to make use of its gearbox in the Liberty-engined machine. I suspect that the Barlow Benz returned to Germany.

Having disposed of the achievements of these 200 hp Benz cars, there remains the problem of their identity.

From records in my possession I can confirm that the Hemery car of
1909 was that driven in 1922 by Zborowski and broken up in 1923. The
same source tells me that the car raced sensationally by Barlow in 1922
was the ex-Hornsted car. Hornsted has stated that he never saw his car
again, but from the aforementioned letter that he wrote to *The Autocar* in
1922, it seems that he recognised that Barlow had his old car. He probably
did not actually see it because, after racing an army-surplus Dodge and
trying to tame the V12 Sunbeam for Coatalen in 1921 (when he also drove
the long-wheelbase 4-seater Benz), 'Cupid' — after an unhappy experi-

*This Blitzen-type Benz
can be seen in the
Daimler-Benz Museum
at Stuttgart.*

ence with a mysterious small car called a Summers — appears to have kept away from Brooklands for most of the 1922 season. My records suggest that the touring Benz raced by Roberts in 1920, Hornsted in 1921, and Miller and his associates from 1928 to 1930, were one and the same. There remains the problem of the identity of the fine Blitzen Benz in the Daimler-Benz Museum at Stuttgart. This looks very like the Hornsted/Barlow car. The steering wheel is, I think, lower, more like that on the cars that went to America, and there is fairing round the exhaust stubs. The wire wheels are covered by discs. The colour is also aluminium instead of white, but all these alterations to what could be the Hornsted/Barlow car could be explained when it is remembered that the car would have had to be tidied up after Duff's accident, when Mercedes-Benz decided to add it to their collection. After correspondence with Daimler-Benz in Stuttgart and two visits to their excellent Museum there, the last in 1962, I am convinced that Zborowski had the Hemery car and that Barlow raced the ex-Hornsted Benz, the latter probably the one rebuilt for display in the Stuttgart Museum.

7. The Mercedes Element

In the early days particularly, Mercedes cars were prominent and successful at Brooklands. Indeed, at the very first meeting there, on 6 July 1907, in the 30½-mile First Montagu Cup race, the famous Dario Resta, driving F. R. Fry's 1906 Grand Prix Mercedes, should have won at a canter but he failed to recognise the semaphore signal at the Fork instructing him to turn into the Finishing Straight on the last lap. He continued round the outer-circuit, coming home third, losing for his entrant the first prize of 1,400 sovereigns and the Montagu Cup valued at 400 sovereigns.

The race winner was J. E. Hutton in another of these four-cylinder 175×150 mm (14,452 cc) Mercedes, who averaged some 82 mph for the distance, in spite of one cylinder being out of action towards the end. Hutton beat the Japanese Prince K. Okura on his 120 hp Fiat. Resta put in a protest that he was waved round again by an official in spite of having kept a

The Mercedes with which Lautenschlager won the 1908 French Grand Prix at Dieppe. Several of these GP Mercedes appeared at Brooklands' races after their road-racing days were over.

count of the laps he had completed. But the BARC held that the Fork signal was working properly, so the top prize money was lost.

These two big Mercedes of the team, driven in the French Grand Prix by Camille Jenatzy, Vincenzo Florio and Mariaux, finishing 10th and 11th, were to become a feature of the Weybridge Track for some time to come. Indeed, during that first season at Brooklands, Mercedes cars won more prize money than any other make, to the tune of £2,800 in 1907 currency. With the temporary cessation of the French Grand Prix after 1908, the victorious Mercedes cars (with one of which Lautenschlager had won at 69 mph that year in the 477-mile contest at Dieppe) were of little further use to Mercedes in Germany, and two of these 154.7×170 mm (12,781 cc) cars came to England to be raced at Brooklands, one bought by Fry for Resta to drive, the other by Gordon Watney for Lord Vernon. Watney ran a business in Weybridge at which he converted old closed-bodied Mercedes into very smart and fast Gordon Watney open sporting cars, which he also entered for Brooklands races. Most of these were the Sixty and Ninety Mercedes, the engine size of which precludes them from this book. But the two Grand Prix cars from that race which was such a fine victory for the make, became frequent competitors and well-liked at the Track, Fry passing his on to A. W. Tate. It is difficult now to determine exactly which car was which. In fact, there were so many different Mercedes racing at Brooklands between 1907 and 1914 that it was suggested a book could be devoted to them, and that if they did not appear they would be badly missed.

They provided thrills of their own. For example, at the Easter 1908 races Resta was leading Frank Newton on the 90 hp Napier in the race of that designation, and as Newton began to pass Resta his car slipped down the banking on the damp surface. The two cars were locked together momen-

All that remained of C. Lane's Mercedes after it had left the Member's banking at the 1908 BARC August Meeting. The mechanic died from his injuries.

Another view of the ill-fated Mercedes. The car on the track is thought to be the BARC's Sizaire-Naudin, which would have gone to the scene of the accident.

tarily, the Napier losing spokes from its wire wheels and the Mercedes's hub cap being wrenched off. Again Resta lodged a protest, that Newton had been driving too high up the banking for his speed, but it was not upheld. Previous to that there had been the ghastly accident at the 1908 August Meeting, when C. Lane, driving Burford's 76 hp Mercedes in the

Aftermath of the disaster — the engine of Lane's Mercedes was flung some eight feet after tearing itself out of the chassis.

One of the many Mercedes which were such a feature of the Brooklands meetings in the early days.

The 1906 Grand Prix Mercedes owned by F. R. Fry and raced for him at Brooklands by Dario Resta, who is behind the wheel. Later A. W. Tate owned this Mercedes.

100-mile O'Gorman Trophy race, had something go amiss, causing the car to dive off the Members' banking where it crossed the River Wey. The Mercedes, which was estimated to have been travelling at about 97 mph, hit a parapet of the bridge, which ripped out the engine and dumped it on the river bank. The mechanic, William Burke, was flung out of the car, and died soon afterwards. It may be that after long road races these big cars

were beyond the first flush of youth, because in 1909 Resta had the steering fail on the GP car, but pulled up safely.

As I said in the Introduction, there is little point in describing in detail
the individual races in which the bigger cars competed at Brooklands in
those early times, because exciting as such cars were, they were less
noticeable then than in later days when they stood out among lesser
machinery. But the Grand Prix Mercedes had long and honourable careers
there.

Lord Vernon's 1908 GP car was given a radiator cowl and a streamlined
tail. It is not easy to decide which of the big Mercedes was which after this
lapse of time, nor their sequence of ownership, but Tate was still running
his 1908 Mercedes at Shelsley-Walsh hill-climb in 1913, where it established a tiny facet of history by hitting the railings and pulling off the dust
cover from its nearside front wheel, which was then replaced with a loaf
of bread of the round kind then current! This is thought to have been the
winning 1908 GP Mercedes, which after the war went to America, where
it was meticulously restored by George Waterman, and by 1909 E. H.
Turnbull was entering one of these cars for Resta to drive; and Lionel
Mander and Noel Macklin also ran them. Lord Vernon was still entering
his, as was Tate, in 1911.

These old road racing Mercedes were fast, Resta doing the standing-
start 10-mile and flying-start half-mile distances in 1908 at 89 and 95.5
mph respectively, and later improving the half-mile figure to 100.84 mph
(using, it is thought, the spare car for the 1908 Grand Prix, with the 13.1-
litre engine) and later he lifted the half-mile record to 103.15 mph, lapping
in the process at 102.01 mph. The following year Laurent's 1908 GP
Mercedes increased the flying-start kilometre record to 105.29 mph, then
improved this to 107.86 mph, and took the class half-mile record to 109.05
mph. I believe he had used up two engines by that time. His car established the fastest lap in a 1911 BARC race, at 101.43 mph.

The popularity of these Mercedes cars caused the BARC to give them a

*J. Hartshorne-Cooper's
Grand Prix Mercedes
outside the Track
garages. On the right is
George Bedford's
racing Hillman, with a
Speed Model Hillman
beside it.*

Capt. Jack Hartshorne Cooper's old Mercedes returns to the paddock after winning a race in 1920.

race to themselves in 1912. But of the 11 entries only one, Alan Mander's 13,586 cc car, comes into the 'giant' category, and it was a non-starter. By the following season, such Mercedes had ceased to thrill the Brooklands crowds.

J. Hartshorne Cooper in the Mercedes. Capt. Cooper was killed a year later while testing his new aero-engined Cooper-Clerget on the Track.

Preparing the Mercedes for a race. It had been somewhat modified since its Grand Prix days and been given oversize tyres.

After the Armistice, Capt. Jack Hartshorne Cooper entered one of the 1908 GP Mercedes for Brooklands races, possibly the ex-Tate car, which may have been the one with which Willy Poge had driven into 5th place in the Grand Prix, but now with wire wheels and one of the smaller 12,781 cc engines.

He had quite a reasonable amount of success with the old car. In the Private Competitors' Handicap at the 1920 August Meeting he was third, behind the 1912 Grand Prix Lorraine Dietrich which could initially out-accelerate the older GP car, and Count Zborowski's 1914 GP Mercedes. But at the following Essex MC Brooklands Meeting, Count Zborowski lent the Cooper car, won the Essex Lightning Short Handicap at 90.25 mph and it was third in the Essex Lightning Long Handicap. Then, at the BARC Autumn Meeting of this first post-war season, the old Mercedes gave its owner two more third places, in the Lightning Long Handicap and in the Senior Sprint race. By this time the car was presumably getting a bit too slow for Cooper's liking. It was a non-runner at the 1921 Easter BARC racing, and it became known that Cooper was anxious to follow his friend Count Zborowski in having an aero-engined car to race. The result was the 19.7-litre Cooper-Clerget, described in my other book, but sadly it killed its owner in practice before he had a chance to race it.

Long after this, these old Mercedes made spasmodic appearances at the Track but with unremarkable results, their only appeal that of antiquity. Thus, had the Private Sweepstakes at the 1921 BARC Whitsun Meeting not been abandoned, M. Pilette apparently intended to run his 14,913 cc Mercedes, which could have been a 1906 French Grand Prix car with a shorter-stroke crankshaft. Then, in 1924 S. A. Payn entered a mysterious maroon four-cylinder Mercedes of 24,192 cc (185x150 mm) for a 90 mph

In earlier times the Gordon Watney Mercedes, rebodied and tuned-up at Watney's Weybridge works, were a feature of the BARC races. This one, 'The Knut' (painted heliotrope with red Mercedes stars on its tail), was entered in 1914 by Mrs Thelka Duncan and driven by S. E. Kilham. It had a 6.8 litre engine.

A 1908 GP Mercedes, once raced at Brooklands, and now in America.

Short Handicap but, as this, and an eight-cylinder of 15,413 cc (125x157 cc) with black bodywork, entered by S. A. Payn Junior for a Private Competitors' Handicap in 1926, were non-starters, they remain a mystery.

8. Malcolm Campbell's Darracq 'Blue Bird'

The Darracq was a popular make a Brooklands, but apart from the 120 hp model which Warwick Wright drove at the first meeting, the one which qualifies for inclusion here is the 59.6 hp Grand Prix car which Capt. (later Sir) Malcolm Campbell started racing at Brooklands in 1912, with a four-cylinder engine of 155×140 mm (10,507 cc). Those are the dimensions quoted by Campbell when the car was entered for BARC races, but they do not quite add up to those for the Darracqs which competed in the 1906 and 1907 Grands Prix, which were of over 12-litres capacity. The car sounds more like the 1906 Darracq which won the Vanderbilt Cup race in America, but that had a 20 mm larger cylinder bore

Be that as it may, Campbell had a very successful day at the Track when he first appeared with this Darracq, which he had named 'Blue Bird' after Maeterlinck's play — the name Campbell was to adopt for all his subsequent racing and Land Speed Record cars. (Before this he had preferred to call his smaller Darracq 'The Flapper'.)

Appearing at the July 1912 Brooklands Meeting, it won the sixth 100

Capt. (later Sir) Malcolm Campbell's well-known Darracq 'Blue Bird' in its original Brooklands form.

The big 'Blue Bird' Darracq in later form, with streamlined body.

mph Short Handicap from Horniman's Benz and a Gordon Watney Mercedes, with a flying lap speed of 84.7 mph. Campbell was gaily clad in mauve coat and sleeves and dark green cap, in jockey fashion, as still applied to competitors at the Track at this time. He finished the day with

The accident which befell Campbell in 1911 when both offside wheels collapsed as he was running up the Finishing Straight at high speed — but the Darracq was still classed as a finisher!

second place in the Winners' one-lap handicap from the Mercedes. Later that season the big Darracq improved its lap-speed to 90.55 mph, then 92.57 mph, but disaster was narrowly averted on August Bank Holiday in the 100 mph Short Handicap, when, coming up the Finishing Straight, the offside front tyre burst, both offside steel-disc wheels collapsed after striking the kerb and the car skated along for a very considerable distance, actually finishing fourth in this condition, before Campbell pulled it up. Naturally, it did not start in the '100 Long', but it was out again at the Autumn races, lapping at 91.38 mph; and Campbell ran it again in 1913 (with new cylinders, I believe) heavily handicapped and starting his pursuits from the scratch mark, as he had done the previous year.

Nevertheless, at the Easter 1913 Meeting the Darracq managed third place in the Private Competitors' Handicap, with a lap at 92.57 mph and another third place in the 100 mph Short Handicap, its best lap up to 93.62 mph, and yet another third in the Easter Sprint Handicap, which suggests that it possessed good acceleration as well as a maximum speed of around 100 mph, on its high top gear of 1.25-to-1. Malcolm Campbell used it on the road, finding that after he had fitted an SU carburettor it would throttle down to about 18 mph on that high top speed.

9. Humphrey Cook's 100 hp Isotta Fraschini

Humphrey Cook, who after the 1914/18 war raced with considerable success a Ballot and his 30/98 and TT Vauxhall cars, named *Rouge et Noir*, and who later in his career financed the English Racing Automobile project to the tune of nearly £3 million of his own money (occasionally taking the wheel of one of these ERAs) commenced his motor racing at Brooklands with one of the Italian 100 hp Isotta Fraschini cars.

The car with which Cook made his Brooklands racing debut was a standard model Isotta Fraschini endowed with racing bodywork — the Type KM 100 hp which had made its debut at the 1910 Paris Salon. Designed by Giustino Cattaneo, it followed the specification of previous Isotta Fraschini racing cars in having its valves prodded by an overhead-camshaft, but on this production chassis the valve gear was enclosed in an aluminium casing. Twin high-tension magnetos provided dual ignition, a four-speed gearbox with direct drive on the fourth speed was used with chain final drive (the chains encased), and the advanced four-wheel brake system designed by Oreste Isotta Fraschini, brother of Vincenzo Fraschini (which system this make had pioneered), was fitted, with a transmission brake for good measure.

This Type KM Isotta Fraschini cost £1,200 in England, and one of the customers was Lord Vernon, who had raced a 1908 Grand Prix Mercedes at the Track. The impressive 100 hp Isottas had a four-cylinder 130×200 mm 10.6-litre engine with four overhead valves per cylinder operated by a vertical-shaft-driven overhead camshaft. Lubrication, however, was by troughs and dippers. This exciting motor car was said to have a power output of 140 bhp at 1,800 rpm, and a top speed of 90 mph, and as presumably it had brakes in keeping, it must be regarded as a very significant fast car of the Edwardian years. The chassis weight was just over 46 cwt. In fact, it did not go into production, and then only in small numbers, until 1911. Some say that only 10 of these great cars were built between then and the outbreak of the war that killed off such Edwardian grandeur and turned the KM's designer to aero-engines.

For Brooklands, in 1914, Cook's Isotta Fraschini retained its front-wheel brakes, and the chain-drive chassis was given the usual pointed-tail body, painted black with red bands, and a radiator cowl. It made its debut at the 1914 Whitsun Meeting, in the second heat of the Private Competitors' Handicap. It was flagged away last, the handicappers taking no chances with the newcomer, with its 10,618 cc engine. A bad bout of misfiring resulted in a lap-speed of only 71.73 mph, the car only picking up on each lap at the end of the Railway Straight. Out again for the 16th 100 mph

Short Handicap, Cook found himself sandwiched between two Mercedes, and giving four seconds to Dewis's Sixty which, like the Isotta, was rated at 41.9 hp. Although the lap speed was up to 78.55 mph this was insufficient to gain a place. In the 100 mph Long Handicap, Cook had to give Dewis's Mercedes a six-second start, and the apparent ignition trouble made his car slower than before.

At the Summer Meeting it was evident that Humphrey Cook had got the measure of his big car, and although it was on the scratch mark in the Private Competitors' Handicap it lapped at a best of 91.38 mph, fastest in the race, and finished second to Capt. Lindsay Stewart's 3-litre Schneider. In the 100 mph Long Handicap at this meeting it went even better, its quickest lap being at 92.06 mph, taking third place. Then, in the 100 mph Short Handicap it pulled out a lap at 92.74 mph, proving that it was a genuine 100 mph car, and won from the Straker-Squire and the Schneider, at 87.34 mph, discomforting the 'bookies' who had quoted odds of 10-to-1, usually reserved for non-finishers! Presumably they thought Cook would require more distance in which to work up speed.

Cook ran the Isotta at the Inter-Varsity Brooklands Meeting, but had to be content with third place in the One-Lap Handicap behind Lionel Martin's little Singer and an Austin, because he missed a gear-change going on to the Home banking, but he nevertheless averaged 77.03 mph for the standing-start lap. Running in the Two-Lap Handicap he made no such mistake, gaining the Isotta Fraschini's second Brooklands win, from a fast Vauxhall and a baby Mathis. Cook had little time left in which to enjoy the sport pre-war, and although he drove the car again at that fateful 1914 August Bank Holiday Meeting, it was down on speed and non-started in the last race for which it was entered. Cook had also tried his hand with the car in hill-climbs and sand racing, running at the 1914 Lancashire AC's Waddington Fells event, where the car's undershield came adrift, and at Saltburn that year, where it won on handicap. It did not reappear again after the Armistice.

Humphrey Cook, better remembered for his generous sponsorship of Raymond Mays's ERA project, started his motor racing at Brooklands in 1914 with this 10.6-litre chain-drive Isotta-Fraschini.

10. The 1912 Lorraine-Dietrich 'Vieux Charles Trois'

One of the best-loved and longest-lived Brooklands cars was the 1912 Grand Prix Lorraine-Dietrich 'Vieux Charles Trois', brought there after the war by Capt. Malcolm Campbell. It had many drivers and was still active in 1929. In this picture Douglas Hawkes is 'up'.

This 1912 15-litre Grand Prix Lorraine-Dietrich had a competition career extending over 27 years, and in the 1920s was one of the more popular cars that was raced by a number of different drivers in the BARC short-handicap contests.

One of the last of the giant cars built for Grand Prix racing, it is an impressive motor car by the standards of the present day. It was built by La Société Lorraine des Anciens Etablissements de Dietrich et Cie de Lunéville at Argenteuil near Paris, for the 1912 French Grand Prix, for which race a team of four of these great cars was prepared. de Dietrich had run cars in the 1907 and 1908 French Grands Prix, and when this classic race was revived after a lapse of four years, this long-established engineering concern was again anxious to be represented. However, it had failed to recognise the progress made in racing-car design in the interim and, with Fiat, built giant-engined cars which were unable to compete with the smaller high-speed engines of other competitors, such as Peugeot whose comparatively diminutive 7.6-litre twin-overhead-camshaft, Henry-inspired racing car won at 68.4 mph and spelt the death-knell of the over-engined machines. But, while Fiat at least used an overhead-

camshaft engine, the Lorraines relied on old-fashioned push-rod ohv
engines of even larger dimensions than those in the Fiats. It has been suggested, in fact, that they did not make these engines themselves but sub-
contracted them from Benz in Germany, and certainly in cylinder dimensions and design the engine of the 1912 Lorraine-Dietrich seems to owe a
great deal to the 150 hp engines which powered Benz racers as early as
1909.

I cannot confirm that this is true, but it could be significant that before it
embarked on automobile manufacture de Dietrich et Cie were situated at
Lunéville in Lorraine, so that they had Teutonic connections. Moreover,
they appointed Hemery, Harris and Heim drivers for three of their GP
cars, all of whom had had experience of Benz racing cars in earlier years.
Could it be that these men had advised the French factory about its 1912
racing cars? On the other hand the story that Lorraine-Dietrich never
made its own engines seems to be discounted by the fact that their designer Marius Barbarou was soon to be responsible for some advanced
Lorraine aero-engines that, like the 155x180 mm GP cars of 1908, had been
notable for overhead valves inclined at 45°. If they did employ outdated
Benz engines for the 1912 GP this must surely have been merely a matter
of expediency. Certainly Karl Ludvizsen, in his splendid history of the
Mercedes and Benz racing cars, reminds us that the Benz designer
returned to France in 1911 to join Lorraine-Dietrich, and that when this
firm unveiled its entries for the 1912 French Grand Prix the cars were seen
to be astonishingly exact replicas of the 1908 Grand Prix Benz, apart from
the contours of the bonnet.

These Lorraines owed their performance to brute force, consisting as
they did of a huge engine in a short-wheelbase chassis frame with no pre-

*An evocative
Brooklands scene. Cars
going out for the start
of a 1921 100 mph
Short Handicap race,
with the venerable
Lorraine-Dietrich on
the right of the picture,
and a GP Vauxhall to
its right.*

tence of streamlining, although it has been remarked that for their engine size they were comparatively low cars. The engine was a four-cylinder of 155×200 mm, giving a capacity of 15,095 cc. The cylinders were cast in pairs, each pair weighing 80 lb., with heads integral with them. The 3 in. valves were in the heads, the inlets in cages on the offside, the exhausts on the opposite side and spaced more widely, so that longer (8$^1/_4$ in.) rockers were needed to actuate them than for the inlet valves. Push-rods some 20 in. long rose from the crankcase on the offside and were united to the rockers by yokes and pins. There were two sparking plugs per cylinder set in the offside of the heads and another single plug per cylinder on the nearside, fired by two Fellows magnetos. These magnetos were mounted on the offside of the crankcase and driven by two shafts extending rear-wards from the timing case — the front magneto being driven by the upper shaft, the rear magneto by the lower shaft, via the centrally-located water pump. From this pump a four-branch pipe delivered water to the base of each cylinder, the outlet consisting of a two-branch pipe from heads to radiator. I think that originally there was a cooling fan. The pistons were cast-iron.

On the nearside of this huge power unit the carburettor was set very low down, feeding through a 2$^1/_2$ in.-diameter Y-shaped inlet manifold. Four 3$^1/_4$ in.-diameter exhaust pipes dropped vertically from the exhaust ports, these now entering a cylindrical Brooklands expansion chamber with a 2$^3/_4$ in.-diameter tailpipe. Amongst these pipes rose two big copper breathers. The engine was mounted in the frame in a channel-section cradle. An Albert Léfevre sight-feed lubricator and hand pump occupied some of the under-scuttle space, but there were no instruments.

The chassis had half-elliptic front springs shackled at the back, and a back axle consisting of a single I-section beam on half-elliptic springs shackled at both ends and located by tubular radius arms. Tape-and-coil-spring shock-absorbers were apparently used, and the car was steered by a four-spoke alloy steering wheel having two hand controls on a quadrant above it and two minor control levers on the column.

Final drive was by exposed 1$^3/_8$ in. × $^3/_4$ in. side chains, and the centre-lock wire wheels, a feature of the 1912 race, carried 34 in. × 4$^1/_2$ in. Michelin tyres. There was gravity feed from a 42-gallon cylindrical tank, with two huge filters, strapped down behind two seats which comprised the body-work. The right-hand gear lever worked in a gate inside the body and rear-wheel brakes were applied through cables by an outside hand lever, a transmission brake being applied by a foot pedal. The wheelbase was approximately 9 ft. and there is a crab-track of about 1$^1/_2$ in.

These Lorraines were certainly impressive, if out-dated cars; they had a maximum engine speed of about 1,400 rpm.

The 1912 French GP was a two-day race over a circuit at Dieppe. At first the great Lorraine-Dietrich racers did well, Hemery finishing the first 48-mile lap in third place, behind a Fiat and Boillot's 'small' Peugeot, with Heim fifth. On lap 2, however, both the faster Lorraines, those of Hemery and Heim, retired with cracked cylinders, a trouble which dogged the car in later days, as you will see. Is it stretching surmise too far, I wonder, to suggest that if the engines were Benz they might have been old units supplied to Lorraine from obsolete stocks, so that the cylinders were in none too good a condition at the start of the race?

Be that as it may, although the other Lorraines (driven by Hanriot and

Bablot) continued — the latter working up to fourth place by lap 4, behind the now-leading Peugeot and two Fiats — the fact remains that at the end of the tenth lap and the first day's racing Bablot, too, had retired, and although Harniot had finished tenth out of 26 finishers his Lorraine-Dietrich failed to start the second day's racing; suggesting that its cylinders had also become porous.

Although the 1912 Grand Prix appearance of the 15-litre Lorraine-Dietrich cars was unimpressive, the cars were not entirely wasted. The Grand Prix had been held late in June, and before Brooklands closed for the winter, Victor Hemery, who seems to have been the team-leader, had brought one of the cars to this country. With it he took a number of world and Class J International records, averaging 97.59 mph for one hour and 86.36 mph for six hours, the shorter records, like the 10-laps and 50 miles, being taken at over 101 mph. It is interesting that, in all, Hemery drove just over 518 miles, because the greatest distance that one of these cars lasted in the Grand Prix was 480 miles. It would be interesting to know whether fears for the Lorraine's reliability or the shortness of the late November day caused Hemery to stop after six hours, because had he continued he could seemingly have wiped up several more world records, as these were held, by Sunbeam, at a good 10 mph under Hemery's speed. The Lorraine was entered by W. M. Letts who, with Charles Jarrott, held the Lorraine-Dietrich agency in this country. By taking the world hour record the fiasco of the Grand Prix was to some extent overcome. Szisz then won the 1914 Anjou GP in one of these cars, but he is said to have carried three passengers, so apparently a touring body had somehow been fitted.

However, the last had not been heard of the 1912 GP Lorraine-Dietrich. Malcolm Campbell, searching after the Armistice for a suitable car with which to continue his Brooklands career, found one of these cars in France and brought it to England; the story being that, despite an import ban, he got it into the country by claiming it was an army staff car used during the

The Ellison brothers in their old Lorraine, which they raced in the mid-1920s. The Members' banking forms a backdrop.

war. This may not have been so mythical as Campbell's friends thought, as there is evidence that brackets were fitted on the scuttle for carrying oil lamps, so this old Lorraine may indeed have been used on the road to serve its country during the Kaiser conflagration.

At all events, Campbell entered it for the first post-war Brooklands meeting. Who drove this particular car in the Grand Prix is uncertain, but it was car No. 4, and Heim drove Lorraine-Dietrich IV at Dieppe. Whether it was the car driven at Brooklands before the war by Hemery, I have been unable to ascertain — the plate on the engine says '75 hp type GP No. 4' and the Brooklands records do not reveal the number of Hemery's engine. There is also the number 4241 on one of the cylinders, and as Hornsted's 150 hp Benz of 1909 had engine No. 5100 this could be taken as (very slender) evidence that the Lorraine's engine was made by Benz around 1908. Incidentally, why the makers called this a 75 hp engine is obscure, because the RAC rating was 59.6 hp and the maximum hp should have been higher than 75, the 1908 12-litre GP Itala giving around 100 bhp, while Benz claimed 150 hp from their 15-litre engine.

However, let us gloss over these red herrings and study the old car's Brooklands career. Campbell called it 'Blue Bird'. He kept it in 1912-trim except for sweeping the exhaust stubs into a long pipe extending to beyond the back axle, to comply with Track regulations. The Easter 1920 racing, organized by the Essex MC, was spoilt by rain, but Campbell was persuaded to run a match race against Major Woodhouse on an eight-valve Matchless-MAG motor cycle. The Lorraine won easily, covering a lap at 78.9 mph. When the rest of the races were run off on the following Saturday, the Lorraine won again, at 85 mph — after Bedford's Hillman had mistakenly done a lap too many while in the lead — and Campbell was third in the Final.

When Brooklands put on a full-scale Whitsun Meeting to celebrate its
return to activity, Douglas Hawkes had taken over the Lorraine for its
new owner, the Hon. H. M. Upton. He started from scratch in the Private
Competitors' Handicap but retired with choked jets. However, he made
amends in the 100 mph Short Handicap, winning by 4.4 sec. at 91 mph
having soon overtaken the entire field. In the 100 mph Long Handicap
Hawkes started in a bunch of cars, 6 sec. ahead of Segrave's Opel II. He
went ahead easily and, as Segrave lost a tyre, was never challenged — the
Lorraine, still painted blue, winning at 90.5 mph. The meeting ended with
a two-mile sprint, in which the Lorraine was second to the Opel.

At the 1920 Summer Meeting, Hawkes was unplaced in the '100 Short',
the Lorraine's engine having cooling difficulties, suggesting leaks or a
defective water pump. He ran again, without success, in the '100 Long'.
By August Bank Holiday the old car was itself again, Hawkes gaining
speed quickly after a slow start to win the Private Competitors' Handicap
at 87½ mph from Zborowski's Mercedes. An Essex MC meeting proved
the undoing of the Lorraine, which was wont to indulge in bouts of misfiring and now broke a valve. Repairs had been effected in time for the
Autumn Meeting, when the Lorraine gave Hawkes a win, at 95.18 mph,
from Chassagne's famous 1919 Ballot, in the Lightning Long Handicap, in
which he had 33 sec. start over the French ace. At the September Essex
MC races, Hawkes just failed to catch a Douglas small car in the Long
Handicap, after overtaking Vandervell's Talbot on the inside. In spite of
this excellent season, the Hon. Upton apparently tired of entering the car,
as in October 1920 it was offered 'for quick sale' at £750.

Apparently it found no buyers, and by February the following year the
asking price was down to £500, with 100 mph guaranteed, because
Hawkes himself entered and drove it at the Easter Brooklands Meeting of
1921. He retired from both his races, with choked jets in the first (which
caused a fire as the engine was restarted), and a pin coming adrift from a
valve rocker as soon as it started in the second. Before the Whitsun
Meeting A. R. Pole had acquired the Lorraine. He wisely let Douglas

*Old-car competitor
C. D. Wallbank in the
now-ancient Lorraine,
with which, even so, he
contrived to break Class
A long-distance
records.*

Hawkes go on driving. It was sent off only 14 sec. before Segrave's 4.9 Sunbeam in the 100 mph Short Handicap at Whitsun, but although it averaged 87.78 mph to the Fork from the Pond Start and made its flying lap at 97.08 mph, it failed to beat its handicap and was unplaced. It came out again for the 'Lightning Short' race but managed only 85.69 mph on its standing lap, then retired, the clutch slipping after being 'dressed' with too lavish a dose of oil. It was going well again in time for the '100 Long', accelerating to the Fork at 89.44 mph and doing its flying laps at 102.06 and 104.85 mph, well above handicap, but it was unplaced. Hawkes had a busy day, for he also drove a Horstmann (instead of his Morgan) and now, in the Lightning Long Handicap he got the Lorraine away really well (91.17 mph for its initial lap) but after going round at 103.11 mph, tailed off to 86.17 mph as the engine began to misfire. It non-started in the sprint race.

Before the 1921 Summer Meeting, Pole had the Lorraine repainted bright scarlet, which contrasted well with its brass-bound bonnet. Racing under a blazing sun, with H. M. the King of Spain an interested spectator, Hawkes seems to have hung back, perhaps to assist his future handicap, for the Lorraine's fastest lap in three races was 103.33 mph, and mostly it lapped much slower. This seems to have paid off, for at the August races Hawkes won the '100 Short' for Pole at 93.64 mph, with a lap at 102.48 mph, catching Campbell's Talbot in spite of a modest opening lap. It then went off, rehandicapped from the 'limit' mark in the 'Lightning Short', lapped at a mere 101.43 mph and won at 85 mph from Duff's enormous Fiat. This was too good to last, and after an opening lap at 82.68 mph, Hawkes retired from the 100 mph Long Handicap, but managed a poor third place in the 'Lightning Long', lapping at 96.33 mph. The 1921 Autumn Meeting gave Hawkes a second and a third place, its best lap being 105.97 mph, while its big engine, when in good humour, could dispose of the standing lap at 91.52 mph. Hawkes drove in his famous woollen 'night-cap' and rolled-up shirt sleeves. He had fitted two aero screens and I think he was responsible for the aerofoil fairings on the front axle and steering tie-rod which are still on the car and contrast oddly with the vast expanse of uncowled radiator. The front dumb-irons were also faired-in at this period.

The same arrangement operated in 1922, Hawkes driving for Pole. The Lorraine now wore an even more brilliant coat of red paint, with white wheels. It went so well in the Easter 'Lightning Short' that Chassagne in the V12 Sunbeam finished a mere length ahead of Hawkes, who had a start of 20 seconds. The Lorraine lapped at 102.27 mph. It was unplaced in the '100 Long' and retired from the 'Lightning Long' when a tyre threw a tread. *The Autocar* speculated whether the old car would be faster if properly streamlined, but no-one ever troubled to find out!

The car was absent from the next three meetings. It returned, without success, at the August Meeting, breaking a valve and wrecking a cylinder while going well for victory in the 100 mph Short Handicap. Somehow the damage to this dubious part of the Lorraine's anatomy was repaired and the venerable racer was on form again by the Autumn Meeting, with a lap at 104.85 mph, although unplaced.

About this time someone pointed out that one could have a season's sport at Brooklands for an outlay of £200 by buying an old GP car, and this apparently struck a young man called Alfred Ellison as a good idea, for he acquired the Lorraine, which, for some inexplicable reason, was henceforth known as 'Vieux Charles Trois'. Ellison bravely decided to drive this 'difficult' car himself. He commenced carefully, lapping at under 80 mph, but was exceeding 100 mph in his second race. He was rewarded with two third places.

Alfred Ellison — who lived at Footherley Hall, near Lichfield, which estate he purchased in 1922 — had served in the Royal Flying Corps during the war, and after he had given up racing the Lorraine-Dietrich and driving a Renault 45 at Shelsley-Walsh hill-climb, he became an experienced private pilot, flying his de Havilland Puss and Leopard Moths to Africa and all about Europe, as well as competing in many air rallies accompanied usually by his brother George Ellison, or his wife.

Ellison must have been quite a man, because while practising for the Summer Meeting he experienced a tyre burst as the Lorraine-Dietrich was coming off the Members' banking. The big car slewed round and slid backwards down the banking. It spun again, which tore more tyres from the rims, one cover hitting the mile Timing-box and passing completely through it! Ellison held the car and, although he non-started in his first two races on the Saturday, he came out to win the 100 mph Long Handicap at 96 mph, after a standing lap at 86.61 mph and a best lap of 102.69 mph. In spite of a lap at 103.11 mph the car, driven by Hawkes, was unplaced at the August Meeting — the handicapper had found them out! But at the Autumn Meeting a lap of 103.33 won the 'Lightning Long' for Ellison, at 96.5 mph. He appears to have re-shod the car with Continental cord tyres.

Ellison was sufficiently pleased with his 12-year-old racing car to enter it again in 1924, but although it was as fast as ever, lapping at 105.29 mph during the season, he had to be content with four third places and one second place, this in spite of being absent from the last two Meetings! Rightly *The Autocar* referred to the Lorraine as 'that extraordinary car' and Ellison showed his appreciation of it by bringing it out again for the 1925 season. At the Easter Brooklands Meeting the Lorraine, still painted red with white wheels, non-started in its first race, and its others were scrubbed because of rain. However, at Whitsun it was out again, Ellison starting cautiously, no doubt to fox the handicapper, with a first lap at 87.84 mph, a second lap at 89.25 mph and failing to reappear for the remainder of that day. At the Summer Meeting Hawkes drove again and upped the flying lap to 96.9 mph after a slow start in the 100 mph Short Handicap, then opened right up to 105.97 mph in the 'Lightning Short', which he won easily from the limit mark, at 99 mph. This led to a 15 sec. rehandicap in the next race, when the lap speed fell to 102.48, which, still rehandicapped, Hawkes increased to 103.33 mph for the second lap of the next event, being unplaced in both.

Hawkes again drove for the owner at the August races, and it is to the ancient car's credit that it was on scratch in the 100 mph Short Handicap, giving away 39 sec. to a 1908 11½-litre Napier. Hawkes covered his flying lap at 105.52 mph, finishing second to a modern 20/70 Crossley that had left 19 seconds before the Lorraine. This speed is quite remarkable, especially as the engine was on three cylinders at the end of the race and the car usually carried an intrepid passenger — including, on one occasion, John Cobb. In the 'Lightning Long' Hawkes actually held a TT Vauxhall at bay for most of the distance, both cars being 'swamped' by the backmarkers on the last lap. The best lap this time was at 104.19 mph.

This seems to have been the old car's best Brooklands appearance for some time. For three years 'Vieux Charles Trois' languished at Ellison's baronial home in the Midlands. C. D. Wallbank heard of the old car and decided to buy it as a stable companion to his 1914 TT Humber. After a hectic trial run along the country roads near the Ellison estate he proceeded non-stop to Brooklands, via Oxford, which ranks as one of the epic instances when a racing car has been driven on the public road. Arriving intact without having stalled the engine, Wallbank discovered that the impulse starter didn't work; so thereafter he relied on push-starts. He also had to get used to doing 110 mph or so when the rev-counter indicated a mere 1,400 rpm, while lack of weight over the back wheels called for considerable skill when entering or leaving the Members' banking.

Wallbank entered for the Gold Vase race at the 1929 Whitsun Meeting and received a favourable handicap. He did his opening lap at 85.87 mph and took the lead, when the throttle control broke and he came to rest. He did not run in the next race. Although repainted blue, the Lorraine was posted a non-starter for the rest of the season, Wallbank being too busy with his 1914 TT Humber (which won its race at the August Meeting) to pay much attention to 'Old Charles'. He had, however, the ambitious idea of attacking the Class A 200 mile and 200 kilo records with the old car, and set about preparing it. A two-gallon petrol tin was put in the passenger's seat, and from this oil was fed by a hand pump through a flexible pipe to the sump, to supplement the car's lubrication system — a shot being given every two laps. Two taper-shape Castrol oil tins were mounted upside down on the top of the scuttle, and from these oil was metered to drop on the driving chains. The front dumb-irons were aproned over.

Wallbank's first attempt met with disapproval on account of the noise made by the Lorraine, so the exhaust system was modified. Then, on the next onslaught, the water pump came partially adrift, the engine began to seize, and before Wallbank could stop cracks had developed in the cylinder blocks — the weak feature of this engine.

On stripping it down, Wallbank found one piston crown cracked and a gudgeon-pin score in one cylinder wall. Ever ingenious, this Birmingham enthusiast, who somehow contrived to make a living out of motor racing although his only cars were both of pre-1914 vintage, made up a sal ammoniac and iron solution in which he pickled the cylinder blocks for two weeks, had the damaged piston and cylinder welded, cleaned everything up with emery cloth, and tried again. This time he was rewarded, both records falling to a car now 17 years old, at 82.79 and 80.56 mph, respectively, a top speed of 100 mph being held to allow for a refuelling stop. The repairs had probably cost £2! Later Cobb's V12 Delage relieved the Lorraine of its records.

The Lorraine-Dietrich was entered once more at Brooklands, for the 1930 Whitsun Meeting, but by then such ancient chain-driven machinery was out of favour with the authorities, and Wallbank wasn't allowed to start. There, for the time being, ended the racing career of this astonishing car.

The Lorraine was put in a shed at Brooklands and forgotten. When C. S. Burney took over K. Kirton's veteran car business he found the old car amongst his stock. I saw it and decided that although the VSCC hadn't been thought of, I could have a lot of fun running 'Old Charles' in the

'Vieux Charles Trois' abandoned on the Brooklands aerodrome, circa 1934. It was valued then at about £5.

R. G. J. ('Dick') Nash took pity on the old Lorraine and restored it. It became one of the fastest of the ex-racing Edwardians and is seen here before a Crystal Palace meeting. Nash is in the car, behind which is the 1908 Itala. Nash's mechanic is on the right of the car in overalls; the author, arms folded in raincoat, looks on.

Brighton Speed Trials. I also discovered that there was no Brooklands Class A Mountain-circuit lap record and I was keen to establish this with the Lorraine. The BARC Clerk of the Course assured me that while ancient racing cars were unwelcome at race meetings, because a fatal accident there would result in adverse Press comment, it was up to the

record-attacker if he wanted to kill himself, and so they would agree to time Boddy and 1912 Lorraine! Burney had meanwhile sold the car to the equally-enthusiastic Philip Rambaut of Northampton for £5. He kept it for several months and his brother tinkered around with it, and while he was learning to fly at the Brooklands Aero Club (he later owned the DH Gipsy Moth G-ABBW and joined the RAF and ATA) got it up to about 70 mph on the Track. Having no place in which to keep it, Philip Rambaut sold it to R. G. J. ('Dick') Nash, who had taken over Burney's business (renaming it the Horseless Carriage Corporation, Inc — television sets repaired) and claimed the Lorraine as his. So my ambition remained a day dream and the BARC was spared the need to add my name above that of Sir Malcolm Campbell on the lap-record plaque on the Clubhouse wall!

However, Dick Nash did more for this historic motor car than I could have done. When he gave me an exciting ride in it along the Brooklands aerodrome roads in 1934 it was in a sorry state. By now someone had painted it black. Nash set about restoring it, removing Brooklands oddments and painting the car its national blue, with the cross of Lorraine on the big radiator, to get the car back into French Grand Prix trim. As a precaution, he fitted guards over the driving chains.

When the Crystal Palace circuit was opened in 1937, Nash indulged in a match race with Clutton's 1908 Grand Prix Itala, which he won. Then, at the VSCC Croydon Speed Trials the Lorraine broke a piston. This put it into retirement, but Nash rebuilt it and showed the car to be capable of lapping the Crystal Palace track at 48 to 49 mph, and clocking 24.5 sec. at Lewes. Indeed, with the possible exception of Heal's S61 Fiat and the somewhat modernised 1913 $21\frac{1}{2}$-litre Benz it was one of the fastest of the Edwardian racing cars in VCC and VSCC events.

During the war the Lorraine escaped damage when Nash's Brooklands

Dick Nash in full cry in the revived 1912 Lorraine-Dietrich 'Vieux Charles Trois'. His son has since lent it to the Brooklands Museum.

hangar was bombed. When Vickers-Armstrong closed the Track it was kept in a special shed in the garden of Nash's house in Weybridge, but he loaned it to the Montagu Motor Museum. After Nash's death, his son Richard had possession of the old car, and in 1986 he was persuaded to bring it to the Brooklands Society's Reunion at the Track. With a running start it climbed the Test Hill, but there was evidence that it was still suffering from the maladies which had almost dogged Wallbank's exploits with it, and although it was entered for the 1988 VSCC Prescott hill-climb it was again in trouble and failed to make a climb. When Richard Nash moved away from Weybridge he let the Brooklands Museum exhibit the old Lorraine, a car with a long and exciting career at the Track. It is certainly an outstanding survival from a sterner age, and I hope sincerely that its huge cylinders have not rumbled their last war-cry.

11. The Tipo S61 Fiat

After Lautenschlager had won the French Grand Prix in 1908, this classic race was not held again until 1912. According to some historians this was because the French did not wish to suffer another defeat at the hands of foreign competitors, and according to others it was because France, although having no objection to defeat at the hands of long-established firms, could not stomach the possibility of one of the comparative newcomers to racing — such as Hispano-Suiza or Delage, which had been doing so well in voiturette races — winning the Grand Prix.

So, the 1909 Grand Prix was abandoned because of lack of entries, but not before the rules had been drawn up, stipulating a bore not exceeding 130 mm for four-cylinder engines. Fiat, apparently, expressed great disappointment that the race would not take place, although they do not appear to have put in an entry. However, there seems little doubt that they were preparing a team of cars, because in 1911, when the substitute Grand Prix de France was run at Le Mans by the AC de l'Ouest, they won it with a solitary 130×190 mm Fiat. Apparently, this car (which averaged 56.71 mph, driven by Victor Hemery, and set a lap record of 67.75 mph) did not look particularly like a racing car; the explanation being that the 1909 engine had been put into a normal touring chain-drive chassis. I have heard that the AC de l'Ouest was desperate for entries for this 1911 Le Mans substitute for the cancelled French Grand Prix, and that Ernest Lhoste, the Fiat agent in Paris who seems to have had some influence in the S61 being put into production, put together the Fiat entry. He had to work quickly to get the car ready for the race. Because of a cancelled order, he had a standard chassis in stock and was able to persuade Turin to send one of the S61 racing engines they had prepared for the abandoned 1909 French Grand Prix, for installation therein. He also persuaded test-driver Antonio Fagnano to go as riding mechanic to Victor Hemery. As a late entry, the car was given the number 13, which did not prevent Hemery from winning the race.

In 1911 a Tipo S61 Fiat was sent to America, and with it Bruce Brown won the Savannah Grand Prix at 74.75 mph, which sounds as if this was a proper racing version. The previous year, at Savannah, Nazzaro had broken the lap record on a Fiat before retiring with a broken chain.

The engine of the 1911 Tipo S61 Fiat, which was designed circa 1908/09, is of the utmost interest because it is an overhead camshaft unit, ascribed with hindsight, to the drawing board of Avvocato Carol Cavalli.

When the French Grand Prix proper was revived in 1912, Fiat built some cars for it which were designated Tipo S72, of 150×200 mm. The Tipo

S61 was, however, a production model, and I have seen a claim of 50 sold in three years, although it appears to have been available in England only during 1911. Laurence Pomeroy quoted it as the 90 hp Fiat but, in fact, it was catalogued as the 75 hp, a 90 hp 140x130 mm model having been listed in 1909. I believe these cars were called Tipo 6, the *engine* being S61, but the latter designation is now applied to the cars themselves.

The engine was a departure from previous Fiat practice. It had a capacity of 10,087 cc and two valves per cylinder. There was an inlet and an exhaust valve on each side of the head, permitting a common inlet and exhaust cam but complicating the porting system, so that each valve had one port cored through the head and another fed direct to the manifolding. The valves were actuated by a single overhead camshaft driven by a vertical shaft and bevel gears at the front of the engine. Each valve was held in a detachable cage, the valve being ground to the cage seating and the whole assembly being pulled down on to a copper-asbestos washer. Each cam was separately machined and keyed to the camshaft, and engaged a roller centrally mounted on a bridge-piece coupling a pair of valves.

A Fiat vertical carburettor fed into a curved riser pipe leading to a copper T-shape manifold some 30 in. in length. The Y-shape exhaust manifold obtained some extractor action from the exhaust impulses. A cross-flow cooling system was activated by a water pump driven by a cross-shaft at the front of the engine, the opposite or offside of this shaft driving a Bosch high tension magneto with a twin-brush double-track distributor feeding two plugs per cylinder, one on each side of the head. Full pressure lubrication was applied to bearings, camshaft and valve gear.

The cylinder blocks were bolted to a split aluminium crankcase,

Capt. John Duff with the 10-litre Fiat he found in a London garage.

*Another shot of the
aged Fiat, here seen in
the Brooklands
Paddock.*

attached by four bearer arms, and originally cast-iron pistons were used, while the three-bearing crankshaft ran in white metal bearings.

A cast-iron flywheel 22 in. in diameter enclosed a 72-plate Hele-Shaw type clutch and possessed fan-like spokes to assist in extracting hot under-bonnet air. The drive went to a separate four-speed gearbox with ratios of 1.7, 2.6, 4.05 and 6.25 to 1, and final drive from the integral differential unit was by side chains to a back-axle beam located by radius rods.

As raced at Le Mans the Tipo S61 Fiat had a top speed of about 95 mph. The wheelbase was 10 ft. 3 in., the track 4 ft. $8^{1}/_{2}$ in., and Michelin fixed wooden wheels with detachable rims were shod with Michelin 895x135 tyres. The channel-section frame was sprung on half-elliptic springs devoid of shock absorbers, and the brake pedal actuated two separate contracting band brakes, respectively of 9 in. x 3 in. and 7 in. x 2 in., working through the transmission, one being on an extension of the gearbox layshaft and the other between the differential and the outrigger bearing on the offside of the chassis. The handbrake operated $16^{1}/_{2}$ in. by $3^{1}/_{4}$ in. expanding brakes on the back wheels. There was provision for automatic water cooling of both foot brakes, which functioned together. This 1911 Fiat weighed 28 cwt unladen, 33 cwt ready to race and, with no pretence of streamlining could do some 30, 45 and 65 mph in the indirect gears. One of these cars was supplied as a demonstrator to the late E. E. C. Mathis, who was the Fiat agent in Strasbourg (then in Germany) before 1914. It is said to have had a four-seater sporting body upholstered in pigskin, and to have been specially prepared for Mathis, so that its performance was better than standard.

When Mathis began to build cars on his own account he gave up the Fiat agency, and the Fiat was sent to his own concessionaire in London to be sold. I have heard that instructions were issued that nobody was to be allowed to drive the car. If a potential customer wanted a trial run Monsieur Mathis would come over specially to show off the Fiat's paces.

Advertised by the Mathis concessionaires of Brompton Road, London, in *The Autocar* in January 1914 for £800, it was described as the fastest touring car in England, and its original price was quoted as more than £1,330. The car was sold to Sir Frederick Richmond, the Chairman of Debenham Ltd. He cannot have had much use for it from 1914 to 1918, and he agreed to sell it soon after the Armistice.

At least three of these Tipo S61 Fiats had come to England, as fast touring cars, and it was the ex-Richmond car that Capt. John F. Duff unearthed when he wanted to race at Brooklands after the old Track had re-opened following the war. Interviewing him some time before he met with a fatal riding accident, I understood him to say that he found the Fiat at a dealer's, fitted with a four-seater body. It had a fine fish-tail-shaped petrol tank at the back, so Duff had a two-seater body made to suit it. Such a car was advertised for £500 in April 1920 and it could have been this one that Duff purchased. He tried it out cautiously at the 1920 Westcliff Speed Trials, finishing third in the big racing car class, behind a Sunbeam and an Austro-Daimler. The Fiat was then taken to Brooklands, where it was entered, without success, for the Sprint Race at the BARC Summer Meeting.

However, at the 1920 BARC August Meeting, at which the last three races had to be abandoned because of a deluge of rain, the old Fiat won the 20th 100 mph Long Handicap from Vandervell's Talbot (Vandervell of Vanwall fame!) and Campbell's GP Peugeot. In an earlier race the Fiat had proved difficult to start and only got to the starting line at the very last moment. The blocks were porous, a fault Duff circumnavigated by only filling the radiator just before he was due to leave the Paddock. He told me a splendid story of how, if the engine was misfiring as he came out from behind the Members' Hill on the first lap he kept both hands on the steering wheel, but if it was on all four he would raise an arm as a signal to his friends that all was well, so that they could rush to any bookmaker prepared to offer odds after the race had started. Already the 10-litre Fiat was something of a handful, especially as the spokes were loose in the wooden wheels, necessitating a bucket of water over them to tighten them up. Scrutineering was not a feature of Brooklands in the 1920s!

At the Essex MC Meeting the same month the Fiat ran badly, but gained 3rd places in Short and Long Lightning Handicaps when other cars retired. Duff tried to obtain spare blocks from Italy, without success, but was able to locate another Tipo S61 engine, and with it he somewhat improved his own.

This paid dividends, for, although again late at the start, Duff won the Lightning Short Handicap at the Autumn Meeting at 91$\frac{1}{4}$ mph, pursued by no less a car than a 1919 straight-eight Ballot driven by Chassagne. Had it not been for taking the home banking rather too high on his first lap, Chassagne might have caught the Fiat, for he had devoured the half-mile at a shade under 120 mph. The Fiat, with its two-seater body and external gear and brake levers, was late again for the following race, a '100 Long', and although it travelled almost at the top of the banking it failed to hold its initial speed — indeed, it had slowed perceptibly along the Finishing Straight in winning the previous event.

At this time the car had an undershield under the engine only, the flywheel being exposed, which made it appear quite spidery; subsequently Duff fitted a full-length undershield.

The following year John Duff decided to race the old Fiat again. The Easter Brooklands Meeting took place at the end of March and, in spite of a cold wind, a big concourse of spectators arrived, for Count Zborowski's still-legendary 'Chitty-Bang-Bang' was one of several attractions on the race card. But Duff's Fiat was not to be denied. Starting from the 26 sec. mark in a field of five in the Lightning Short Handicap, and perhaps improved by new engine parts, it lapped at 82.53 mph and then at 96.15 mph, caught Cooper's ancient Mercedes, but was passed by 'Chitty' to finish second to the famous Count. Trouble then returned to plague Duff, the red Fiat missing the 'Lightning Long'.

Duff had discovered an even bigger Fiat, and was industriously arousing 'Mephistopheles' from a long sleep. However, he took both Fiats to Brooklands for the Whitsun BARC Meeting, and must have worked on the Tipo S61 as well, because this car had broken its gearlever getting away from the start of a 100 mph Long Handicap at an Essex MC Meeting the previous weekend, besides misfiring throughout the race.

At Whitsun the smaller of Duff's pair of Fiats finished third from 32 sec. in the 'Lightning Short', lapping at 82.53 and 97.46 mph, and then comfortably won the equivalent long handicap at 97½ mph from the 'limit' mark, its lap speed up to 89.27, 104.19 and 100.82 mph for the respective laps. To round off a good day, and as compensation for 'Mephistopheles' non-starting, the 10-litre Fiat was third in the Senior Sprint Handicap, finishing mere inches behind Campbell's Talbot, although a 3-second re-handicap gave this a start of 14 sec. over Duff.

Duff had both Fiats out at the Brooklands Summer Meeting, and his Tipo S61 was going better than ever before, its radiator enclosed in a bulbous cowl. In the 'Lightning Short' it did its standing lap at 92.92 mph, its subsequent circuit at 102.06 mph, to finish third behind the scratch 'Chitty-Bang-Bang', and in the 'Lightning Long' the car was faster still, lapping respectively at 94.15, 104.41 and 104.85 mph from the 27 sec. mark, which enabled it to overtake a couple of Vauxhalls (a third Vauxhall had retired), to win at 98.65 mph by a big margin. This 104.85 mph lap was the fastest ever done officially by the car in Duff's hands at BARC meetings.

As a change from Brooklands, Duff took the car down to Westcliff in July and drove in the speed trials, his thunderous run netting fastest time of the day — 35.2 sec. for approximately one kilometre. The Fiat was then matched against the fastest motor cycle, Le Vack's V-twin Indian, and won this noisy duel. Duff also entered his Fiat for the Fanöe Island speed trials in Denmark, winning several cups and doing FTD, in 21.69 seconds.

Duff must have been delighted with the car's performance, and porous blocks appeared to have become a problem of the past. At the BARC August Meeting he ran it in the '100 Short' but was on the 4 sec. mark and held his lap speeds down to 72.50 and 80.98 mph. This prevented a penalty in the '100 Long', but the fame of the red Fiat with its black radiator cowl had put it on scratch, and again its driver drove slowly, lapping at 74.56, 88.99 and 83.84 mph, to finish unplaced.

Duff was now so occupied with his bigger Fiat that he disposed of the Tipo S61 to wine importer Philip Rampon. The new owner, who had been racing a TT Humber, later with a Sunbeam aero-engine installed in it, without much success, received a good handicap (30 sec.) in the Lightning Short Handicap at the 1921 BARC Autumn Meeting. Rampon lapped at 86.16 and 96.15 mph but was unplaced. Duff took over for the '100 Short' and was paid the compliment of an 8 sec. re-handicap, but after a standing lap at 87.27 mph the Fiat became sulky and retired, non-starting in the 'Lightning Long'. However, it appeared again, in Rampon's hands, in the '100 Long', but lap speeds of 88.61, 98.62 and 97.65 mph from the 30 sec. mark availed it not at all.

Rampon had the old Fiat repainted white with black wheels, ready for the 1922 BARC Easter Meeting. In the Private Competitors' Handicap it did its standing lap at 70.87 mph and its flying laps at 79.68, 74.92 and 86.17 mph. Perhaps, however, Rampon was anxious not to attract too much attention from the handicappers, for at the 1922 May Meeting the Fiat, now with black cowl and tail, lapped at 85.53 and came home second to the V12 Sunbeam in the Lightning Short Handicap, lapping at 87.25 and 97.65 mph, and leading for most of this race. Rampon was taking no chances with ancient machinery, however, and only entered for the short handicaps.

Rampon had another good day at the Essex MC Royal Brooklands. The Fiat led the Earl of Athlone Lightning Short Handicap from the 57 sec. mark until Cook's straight-eight Ballot passed it as they swept up the Finishing Straight.

The black and white Fiat was present again at the Whitsun races in June. Rampon lapped at 76.14 and 87.99 mph in the Private Competitors' Handicap, but was unplaced, as he was in the '100 Short' although improving his pace to 80.84 and 95.41 mph. Incidentally, Rampon and his passenger went through the race bare-headed, which was quite common at Brooklands in those days.

What Rampon gradually had been working up to, came to him at the BARC August Meeting. The Fiat started from the 35 sec. mark in the

New owner Philip Rampon on the Railway Straight, in the process of winning the 1925 Gold Vase race in the S61 Fiat.

Private Competitors' Handicap, did its opening lap at 86.48 mph, went on to lap at 100.41 mph and won at 93 mph from the 'limit' ABC and Barlow's Bentley. This earned the car a 16 sec. re-handicap in the 100 mph Short Handicap in which it should have started first but now had three cars to pass. Lapping at 85.69 and then at 100.21 mph it ran home third. Coming out again for the '90 Short', Rampon still had a 2 sec. re-handicap to dispose of and, contenting himself with laps at 86.48 and 99.61 mph, he was unplaced.

The Fiat was entered for the Essex MC Championship Meeting in September but failed to appear. However, it was going extremely well at the Autumn Meeting in the Private Competitors' Handicap, being second to Brocklebank's Berliet after going round at 93.87 and 105.29 mph. Re-handicapped, the Fiat failed to complete a lap in the '100 Short', perhaps because Rampon knew exactly how the Brooklands game should be played and didn't wish to be completely out-handicapped in 1923.

By 1923 E. A. D. Eldridge had decided that it would be some time before the rejuvenated 'Mephistopheles' Fiat would be running properly but, having disposed of his Isotta-Maybach to Le Champion, he was left only with a hotted-up Gwynne Eight for Brooklands racing. So he took over the 10-litre Fiat from Rampon. The latter was down to drive the car for Eldridge in the Easter Private Competitors' Handicap and, lapping at 86 and 100.21 mph, finished fifth. The old Fiat, now painted red, appeared in the Founders' Gold Cup Race with Eldridge at the wheel and, starting well from the 18 sec. mark, was pursued by Cook's Vauxhall which, getting off comparatively slowly four seconds later, could not catch the older car. Eldridge won at 96.09 mph, averaging 89.78 mph to the Fork from the Pond start and doing his flying lap at 104.41 mph. It was in this race that Kaye Don only pulled up the Viper by rubbing it along the earth bank below the Test Hill, its brakes proving inadequate — a reminder of the hazards of racing these very fast old cars on the Track. Incidentally, the Fiat was in the same trim, to its cowled radiator and wooden wheels, as

A Paddock shot of the Fiat with the radiator cowl it wore in Duff's time.

when Rampon drove it the previous season, and was on Continental tyres.

So thrilled was Eldridge by this victory that he drove too fast out of the Paddock for the last race of the day, skidded, and burst a tyre. He continued down the Finishing Straight to the start but this caused the cover to fly off the rim, so he was a non-runner. Had he started he would have been sent away with the TT Vauxhall, having been re-handicapped eight seconds. As it was, Cook won at 98.32 mph. The skill of the handicappers is evident in Cook's lap speed of 104.41 mph, for had not the Fiat got round at just this speed in winning the Gold Cup? Had it run, what a close race must have resulted!

At Whitsun, Eldridge relied on the bigger Fiat and his Gwynne, non-starting in all his races. It seems probable that the 10-litre car was proving difficult to prepare, for Mr Brownridge has told us of the long hours he spent trying to maintain compression with valves that were pulling through their cages. However, both the Fiats were entered for the Essex MC Meeting in June, but 'Mephistopheles' did not materialise. Any disappointment Eldridge felt was presumably dispelled by the good showing of the Tipo S61, which gained two third places, respectively in the Senior Short and Lightning Short Handicaps, driven first by its owner, then by Rampon; and was second, Eldridge driving, in the Senior Long Handicap. It is interesting to note that in the last two races the car that finished ahead of the Fiat was Cook's TT Vauxhall. Eldridge non-started in the 'Lightning Long'.

For the BARC Summer Meeting Eldridge at last had his giant six-cylinder aero-engined Fiat ready, so he did not run the smaller car. Philip Rampon gave the Tipo S61 an airing in the '100 Long' at the August Meeting, lapping at 83.42, 94.86 and 93.62 mph, but was unplaced.

Rampon returned to the car for the BARC Autumn Meeting, failing to get to the line for the '100 Short', and being beaten by its old rival the Vauxhall and others in the Lightning Short Handicap, when it lapped at 87.78 and 97.65 mph. Finally, so far as 1923 was concerned, the 1911 Fiat gave Rampon a third place in the Lightning Short Handicap at the Essex MC Meeting at the end of September.

Eldridge being fully occupied in 1924 with 'Mephistopheles' and other things, Rampon took over full control of the smaller Fiat — or perhaps Eldridge had merely shared with Rampon during 1923. At all events, the old car, still painted red, appeared for its fifth consecutive season. It non-started in August but was on form at the Autumn Meeting, only just losing second place to Thomas's Leyland-Thomas in the 100 mph Short Handicap, in which Rampon lapped at 84.41 and 101.43 mph. It retired from the '90 Short', after lapping at 87.61 mph. Late in 1924 Rampon matched the Fiat against two sidecar outfits and a solo motor cycle in an informal three-lap race at an Essex MC Meeting, but finished last.

The Fiat showed no sign of tiring when the 1925 season commenced. Rampon brought it out for the BARC Whitsun Meeting and, finding himself on the limit (39 sec.) mark in the Gold Vase race, proceeded to lap at 90.22 and 103.76 mph, winning at 96.75 mph as Coe's pursuing 30/98 Vauxhall 'Vixen' crashed at the side of the Railway Straight. Rampon having decided that the wooden wheels with their loose spokes were dangerous, the Fiat now had black Rudge Whitworth centre-lock wire wheels, and since 1924, of course, a Brooklands silencer was incorporated in the exhaust pipe that ran along the nearside of the car. This success caused Rampon to be put back to the 'owes 5 sec.' in the 90 mph Short Handicap, but, opening slowly at 87.84 mph, he did his next lap at no less than 103.97 mph, *The Autocar* remarking that 'the ever formidable Fiat was well up in the field.'

Rampon now fades from the Brooklands scene, probably because he had to go abroad in connection with his wine-merchant business, but this did not end the racing career of the old Fiat. It was taken over by Richard Warde, a petrol company representative. The car was still maintained mainly at Parry Thomas's sheds, but sometimes at Harper's garage at Sunbury-on-Thames, from whence it was towed to the Track behind Warde's Chrysler, the mascot of which adorned his son's Standard Vanguard when I interviewed him a few years ago. Warde lived at Cuckfield in Sussex, and many of the Brooklands drivers used to fly down and land in the field behind his cottage. His widow remained there, and quite by chance saw the Fiat pass by on a tow-bar en route for the Brighton Speed Trials one day after the war.

Warde entered his new acquisition for the 1925 Summer BARC Meeting, the car still red with black wheels. In the Lightning Short Handicap he lapped at 93.09 and 104.41 mph, thus proving that he was a fit and proper person to follow in the footsteps of Duff, Eldridge and Rampon, for his fastest lap was but 0.44 of a mph slower than Duff's best-ever speed, and he was placed third on his first appearance. Moreover he co-operated with John Cobb (a driver subsequently to become a holder of the World Land Speed Record, and holder for all time of the Brooklands lap-record) who took over the Fiat for the Lightning Long Handicap. Cobb put up lap speeds of 92.23, 100.61 and 92.40 mph on this occasion and came in third.

This result being very much to Cobb's liking he drove the Fiat in two races at the West Kent Club's Meeting in July, on the occasion of that fantastic Eldridge/Thomas Match Race described in my previous book. Cobb just won the first race from Turner's 2-litre Austro-Daimler, at 97$\frac{1}{2}$ mph, with Howey's 5-litre Ballot hot in pursuit. Then Cobb was beaten by Howey in the third race, finishing second.

Thus 'blooded', Cobb drove the Fiat into first place again at the BARC August Meeting, lapping in the 'Lightning Short' at 94.15 and 109.72 mph from the limit mark, by far the highest speed yet attained. His *average* speed for the race was 101.57 mph. Cobb was re-handicapped from 56 sec. to 40 sec. in the 'Lightning Long' and kept the Fiat down to lap speeds of 94.33, 101.33 and 99.61 mph, to finish unplaced.

At the 1925 Autumn Meeting, starting far back in the field in the '100 Short', for the 1911 Fiat was now generally feared as a very formidable competitor, Cobb completed his opening lap at 95.78 mph, which equalled that of the scratch car, Howey's Leyland-Thomas, then got his unwieldy chain-drive giant round at 110.68 mph. This gave him 3rd place, behind Barclay's TT Vauxhall, which had had a 16 sec. advantage, and Duller's 2-litre Bugatti. Cobb actually gave the larger aero-engined Wolseley Viper six seconds start in the Lightning Short Handicap but washed out its advantage in the first lap, to win at 104$\frac{1}{4}$ mph, his lap-speeds being 97.27 and 112.17 mph. Consistently fast in the old car, Cobb, put back 11 seconds on his published handicap, went round at 97.08, 110.19 and 111.42 mph in the 'Lightning Long', but this was only sufficient to get a fourth place. At the end of the season, Cobb won comfortably the over-2000 cc 8½-mile race at the Essex MC October Brooklands Meeting, the Fiat averaging 107.34 mph.

The 1926 Brooklands season brought further successes for Cobb on the old red Fiat. At Easter he was unplaced in the 100 mph Short Handicap, the Fiat lapping at 98.62 and 102.69 mph, but misfiring. Then, in the Founders' Gold Cup Race Cobb got away slower, at 96.71 mph, but did his fastest lap ever, at 113.19 mph, to finish third, gaining slowly but not fast enough on Barclay's TT Vauxhall that had gone off 8 sec. earlier. This was an excellent speed for a pre-1914 car, faster than many of the aero-engined monsters could manage. Cobb, moreover, went even quicker in the Lightning Long Handicap, lapping at 97.65, 111.92 and 113.45 mph, finishing second to the Vauxhall.

At Whitsun, Cobb was entrusted with Thomas's 'Babs', and in any case, while Warde was practising, the long-suffering Fiat engine broke a piston and literally disintegrated. This seemed the end of the old Fiat's long racing career, but Warde was lucky. During the General Strike of 1926 he happened to discover another Tipo S61 Fiat with touring body engaged in distributing the Government newspaper. After the strike was over, Warde was able to buy the car from its owner, Lord Cunliffe. He used its engine, No. 42, with parts from the earlier engine, to rebuild his racing car. The rebuild seems to have occupied some time, for I can find no trace of the Fiat running again that season — Cobb transferring his affections to an Austro-Daimler. This fortuitous replacement 1911 power-unit was virtually the same as that for which it was substituted, except that it had a water-jacket hot-spot on the inlet manifold made by a firm whose small brass plate announced them to be 'Expert Automobile Coppersmiths'.

Beauty and the Beast!
— the aged 10-litre
Fiat overtaking a smart
3-litre Bentley.

By now Brooklands would not have seemed the same without the Fiat, and sure enough it was back for the 1927 season. At the Easter Meeting Cobb brought it out for the Founders' Gold Cup race, lapping at 93.97 and 102.90 mph, but not gaining a place. He was also driving the single-seater TT Vauxhall at this meeting, but returned to the aged Fiat for the 'Lightning Long', only to retire after lapping at 92.23 and 101.64 mph. By Whitsun the car was back on form, Cobb winning the Lightning Short Handicap at 103.10 mph, with lap-speeds of 95.78 and 110.68 mph. On the Wednesday, rain having washed out the meeting, Cobb lapped at 96.15 and 107.80 mph in the Gold Vase race, but was not successful.

Previous to this, Cobb had won a Surrey Senior Long Handicap at a Surbiton MC Meeting by a ¼-mile from Don's 5-litre Sunbeam, at 104.85 mph. At a subsequent Surbiton MC Meeting, Cobb was engaged to drive Thomas's Leyland-Thomas with its new owner, Mrs W. B. Scott, wedged in the passengers' seat, and in any case the Fiat had refused to start in an earlier race and was left on the starting line.

This brought things to the 1927 August BARC Meeting, but so much rain fell that racing was abandoned, and wasn't resumed as was usually the procedure. To succeed in Brooklands handicaps it was necessary to continually increase speed to outwit the handicappers. It would seem that there was little Warde could do in this direction with a car as old and as well known as his Fiat, but about this time he contrived a new cowl that not only enveloped the Fiat's radiator but also covered the dumb-irons. It seems possible that with modern pistons and fuel the old engine was now developing more than the 120 bhp at 1,650 rpm which Laurence Pomeroy attributed to it in its original state.

Cobb again drove for Warde at the 1927 Autumn Meeting. In the '100 Short' he was on scratch against far more modern cars and, in spite of lapping at 89.09 and 111.67 mph, he didn't get among the first three home. The '100 Long' gave Cobb a very nasty experience, for the steering tie-rod of the Fiat came adrift at over 100 mph. Fortunately the released wheel ran parallel to its fellow and Cobb pulled up safely. The incident happened after the standing lap had been covered at 96.71 mph, so no doubt Cobb was out to win when the steering defaulted.

Cobb was now driving extremely well in a single-seater TT Vauxhall, and the Fiat was put away until 1928.

That this 1911 motor car was still game for racing seven seasons after its first appearance at the Track is remarkable, and certainly its overhead camshaft engine gave far better performance than that of most of the aero-engined monsters — its best lap-speed of 113.45 mph and the great many occasions when it lapped at over 110 mph being notable.

Warde drove the Fiat himself at the 1928 Easter Brooklands Meeting, getting a favourable handicap and going round at 90.06 and 105.52 mph in the Gold Cup race. In the 'Lightning Long' he opened up to 91.89 and 106.42 mph and finished second to Don's 2-litre Sunbeam. At the next meeting Warde retired in the Senior Short Handicap and failed to start in his next race, but the Fiat was back for the August Meeting, when Warde lapped at 95.41 and 105.52 mph in the Lightning Short Handicap. This resulted in the ancient car finding itself on scratch in a field of 15 at the Autumn Meeting, and Warde contented himself with lapping at 93.09 and 105.29 mph in the only race for which he had entered. However, during the season the Fiat chalked up a second place behind Clowe's Buick at a Surbiton MC

Meeting, and at another of these meetings, running high on the bankings so that it baulked faster cars, the Fiat netted another second place.

In 1929 the Fiat turned from racing to record-breaking. It seems incredible that a pre-1914 car should be able to break a record so long after it was built, but the fact remains that, in March, Warde took the British Class A 5-kilometre record at 104.10 mph. It seems that Kaye Don had intended to raise this speed in A. G. Miller's Wolseley Viper, so no doubt Warde kept something in hand. As it worked out, Sir Malcolm Campbell soon put the record well out of reach of even modern racing cars of normal type, by clocking 216 mph in his Napier-Campbell at Verneuk Pan in South Africa.

The Fiat was entered for the 1929 Easter Meeting in the name of G. J. Allday, Warde being nominated to drive it, but it failed to appear. My guess is that after Parry Thomas's death, Warde had to seek fresh stabling for the car, and that Mr Allday found this for him at Weybridge Automobiles. However, old cars were not greatly favoured at Brooklands by 1929, and the gallant old Fiat's racing days were over — for the time being.

It seems, however, that Warde finally left the car at Brooklands, because Thomson & Taylor illustrated the car in one of their 1931 advertisements.

Old racing cars having been banned from the Track, there were no bids, and around 1936 Brian Pickford, who raced ancient big-twin motor cycles at BMCRC meetings, was persuaded by Ken Taylor to take the Fiat away. He paid £6 for it. A trial run round the Track revealed a crack in the cylinder head, which proved difficult to weld. The old car languished for a time in Mr Pickford's garage at Runfold, until a relation, Lionel Roberts, a film actor, took it down to Kent with the idea of using it in a film. A photograph of the car had been published in *Motor Sport*, and Anthony Heal, seeking an Edwardian racing car for the newly instituted VSCC pre-1914

The advanced overhead-camshaft engine of the S61 Fiat.

class, went down to Tatsfield with one of his firm's furniture vans in May 1937 and brought the car home to Buckinghamshire, where it was looked after by Slade's Garage at Penn. The old Brooklands cowling was discarded before the Fiat entered the removal van, and the next task was cleaning up, resetting the camshaft timing and tuning up the engine at Brooklands.

The ancient car reappeared in competition at the 1937 Brighton Speed Trials, when Heal drove it to victory in the Veteran Class, covering the standing start ½-mile at 57.03 mph. Incidentally, Warde was one of the scrutineers and was naturally delighted by the Fiat's victory. En route to Brighton, Heal used to call in at Warde's cottage at Cuckfield with the Fiat to discuss the old Brooklands days.

For the BOC open Prescott hill-climb of 1938, Heal drove the Fiat down under its own power in company with Cecil Clutton's 3-litre Bentley coupé. After two good practice runs of under 58 sec., a valve cotter broke, but Len Gibbs effected repairs. Although this necessitated stripping the entire valve gear, the Fiat was ready in time for the second runs, and despite Heal missing the change-up from 1st to 2nd, the Fiat was placed second to Clutton's 1908 12-litre GP Itala in the Pre-1915 class, the respective times being 58.4 and 59.6 sec.

The next outing was to the Shelsley-Walsh hill-climb, where times of just over 50 sec. were recorded in practice in spite of clutch slip. In the event proper Heal won the Pre-1915 Class in 47.96 sec. from Clutton's Itala (50.98 sec.) and Mavrogordato's 1914 GP Opel (51.17 sec.). On this occasion Michael May's Alvis Silver Eagle towed the Fiat to Shelsley and home again.

Heal went to Brighton again in July 1938, the Fiat winning the Pre-1915 Class. This time it averaged 58.55 mph for the standing-start ½-mile, thus confounding a gentleman who had dismissed its previous time at Brighton as 'impossible' — in spite of the timekeeper's certificate. The actual time was 30.74 sec. and Clutton rode as passenger. This presumably impressed him, because he borrowed the Fiat for the BOC July hill-climb, having towed the old car there from Brighton. On his first run he was caught out by the lack of castor-return action in the steering and left the road for the woods at the first hairpin. Clutton made up for this with a climb in 58.33 sec. on his second appearance, finishing second on formula in the Pre-1915 Class, the Fiat running with mud-wings in place.

Heal then took the car to the VSCC Lewes Speed Trials, where he won the cup for fastest Pre-1915 car, and another for fastest car over 12 years old, his time being 24.8 sec.

At the next BOC Prescott hill-climb, Heal and his Fiat set up an unofficial record for Edwardian cars of 55.91 sec. and won the class both on time and formula.

Returning to Shelsley-Walsh, Heal was unable to practise and lifted off for Kennel Bend but, reaching about 1,500 rpm in 3rd gear, won the Veteran Class with a time of 49.17 sec. On this occasion Heal used his 30/98 Vauxhall to tow the Fiat. It was left at Gretton and ran in the BOC September Prescott hill-climb. Here it won the Pre-1913 Class on time and formula, in 57.49 sec. over a wet course, beating Clutton on a 1912 90 hp Mercedes.

The last active season prior to the war opened with the Stanley Cup Meeting at the Crystal Palace, where the Fiat was on scratch with R. G. J. Nash's 1912 15-litre GP Lorraine-Dietrich in the 3-lap Veteran Handicap

over the Link Circuit. Clutton's Itala, with 12 sec. start, won at 43.7 mph.
The Fiat led the Lorraine away at flag-fall and finished ³/₅ sec. ahead of it
but 3.7 sec. behind the Itala, having averaged some 45 mph.

For the BOC Open hill-climb at Prescott larger-section back tyres were
used to reduce wheelspin. Heal made fastest Edwardian time in 60.48 sec.,
but Peter Hampton's 1910 Bugatti won on formula.

The Fiat's next engagement was an appearance before the BBC's
Emitron TV camera at the Crystal Palace, for a programme called the
'History of Motor Racing'. Besides the Fiat, Nash's Lorraine-Dietrich, a 2-
litre GP Sunbeam, the Opel, Mills's 1907 7-litre Renault and a 1922 ohc
version of racing model-T Ford appeared.

At Shelsley-Walsh in June 1939 Heal clocked 48.49 sec. without having
practised. The larger-section back tyres were used again and the Fiat was
slightly over-geared. However, the Fiat won the Pre-1914 Class from John
Morris's 1913 22-litre Benz (50.77 sec.) and the Itala (51.64 sec.). Next it
was back to the Crystal Palace for the Vintage Cup Race, in which surge
on the right-hand bends caused oil pressure to fall away to zero, but in
which the Fiat finished 3rd from scratch behind Hampton's little 1910
Bugatti, which averaged 39.32 mph, and the Itala. The Fiat averaged 46.75
mph for two laps. Its fastest lap was at 47.7 mph compared to 47.2 mph
for the Itala, and 51.8 mph for the Lorraine, which was on scratch with the
Fiat but started slowly. Heal just passed Shakespeare's Mors on Stadium
Curve, 100 yards from the finish.

The Fiat was taken to Lewes for the VSCC Meeting, where it won the
Pre-1914 Class in 23.52 sec. from Windsor Richards in the Itala (27.13 sec.)
and Hampton in the Bugatti (46.26 sec.) and was also first on formula. In

The Fiat with another form of radiator cowl, as found by Anthony Heal in 1937. He ran it in many VSCC and other suitable events, with commendable success, against such cars as the Itala, Lorraine-Dietrich, and later the Benz; making, for instance, ftd at Shelsley-Walsh, Prescott and Brighton in the pre-1915 class, and racing it at Crystal Palace.

the Unlimited Racing Class Heal was 2nd to Windsor Richards's 5-litre Delage. Peak revs were reached in third gear by the finish, and a bump threw the Fiat all over the narrow road.

Heal entered for the WHDCC Poole Park Speed Trials but, as the Fiat wasn't a sports car and there was no Veteran class, it had to run with the modern racing cars. Moreover, the course was wet, so her acceleration was restricted but she clocked 25.6 sec., beating a 1,100 ERA, a 1½-litre Alta and a 2-litre Bugatti, all of which were supercharged! The Fiat was then towed towards Prescott, getting as far as Marlborough before dark. At Prescott the Fiat beat 19 modern cars to win the Veteran Class on time and formula, setting a new class record of 54.82 sec. At the VSCC Prescott Meeting, Clutton's Itala won the Edwardian Class on formula, but Heal made fastest time, in 62.13 sec., the Itala clocking 64.03 sec. The Fiat was taken to Wakefield's Garage at Worcester to await the Shelsley-Walsh hill-climb, but when this was abandoned because of the outbreak of war, an expedition went down in September 1939 to tow the car home. Unfortunately, between Woodstock and Oxford, the late Peter Roberton Rodger, who was being towed, let his attention wander to some aero-planes and he over-ran the tow bar. The Fiat overturned and his right thigh was broken by the steering wheel.

The wrecked Fiat was left at the Morris Garage, Oxford. It was restored by Easter 1940, the front and back axles, a sprocket and brake drum being carefully straightened and trued up, a new steering wheel fitted and the body panels beaten out — unfortunately the tail had to be shortened.

In March 1941 the old Fiat took its owner to his wedding to Theodora Caldwell at Amersham, the Trade Plate entry under 'Purpose of use' reading 'Getting, and got, married!'

In Heal's hands the Tipo S61 Fiat had achieved notable successes, proving itself the fastest racing car in the Edwardian class, with the possible exception of the more temperamental 1912 Lorraine-Dietrich. In 1946 Heal drove it again at Prescott, clocking 57.25 sec., and at Shelsley-Walsh he won the Pre-1914 Class in 51.21 sec. In his absence, Len Gibbs drove at Brighton, winning his class with a speed of 60.39 mph for the standing-start kilometre.

Anthony Heal leaving the line at the 15 July 1939 VSCC Lewes speed trials in the 1911 Fiat, which made fastest Edwardian Class time. (by courtesy of Graeme Simpson Collection)

Dr G. E. Pinkerton, of Dunstable, took over the Fiat. He continued to race it at VSCC meetings and it has been driven also by Frank Lockhart, whose garage maintained it; but somehow it never regained its former speed. However, the deep rumble of the Fiat's exhaust was one of the loudest and most stirring sounds to be heard at a VSCC race meeting, and I like to close my eyes and imagine I can hear the war-song of this Tipo S61 echoing along the Railway Straight and reverberating from the Vickers sheds, as it did on many occasions between the years 1921 and 1929.

A crack had occurred in the cylinder head of the front pair of cylinders when Warde was racing the car and, although this was welded-up, there was still a troublesome water leak when Anthony Heal was running the Fiat. At Shelsley-Walsh and Prescott hill-climbs he used to drain the water out of the engine after his practice runs and refill the radiator before the timed ascents, as Duff had done at Brooklands all those years ago.

Eventually Heal sold the Fiat to Dr Pinkerton, a VCC member, who had little success with it. He passed it on to a fellow VCC member, Arthur James, who put in hand patterns and a casting for a new cylinder block, but found the machining beyond him. The Fiat Company of Turin were anxious to purchase the car, but the owner didn't want to sell it. So he entered into an agreement with Fiat that they would do the necessary machining and fit the new cylinder block, but that he would have the use of the car during his lifetime, the Fiat becoming the property of the Fiat company on his demise.

However, in spite of repeated visits to Turin, little progress was made, and the work was still uncompleted when Mr James died. So the S61 languishes in the Centro Storico in Turin along with the bigger Fiat 'Mephistopheles'. (See also Appendix 3.)

Wedding carriage! Anthony Heal used the racing 1910 Fiat to drive to and from his wedding at an Amersham Registry Office in 1941, leaving the engine running throughout the ceremony.

12. The 200 hp Benz four-seater

This four-seater Benz with the same four-cylinder 185×200 mm (21,504 cc) engine as the Blitzen-type Benz but with a longer 12-ft. wheelbase chassis and a body by D. & E. Snutsel, Père-et-Fils, of Bruxelles, appeared at Brooklands in 1920.

Thanks to an introduction by Lord Montagu of Beaulieu I was able to meet Harry Quince who had been closely associated with this exciting motor car on its early post-war appearances at Brooklands. Neatly suited and wearing an RFC tie, Mr Quince told me the following story of the big Benz, the car which almost certainly was the same one that Capt. (later Sir) Alastair Miller was to race with considerable success at the Track in later years.

I was glad to be able to chat with Mr Quince, because he was filling in details about a car which I knew had raced at Brooklands but whose early history was a mystery.

The Benz we were now discussing was not one of the Blitzen variety whose separate histories remain so entwined. It was, indeed, a green four-seater with a snout protruding from its radiator and the vestige of a

The versatile Capt. (later Sir) Alastair Miller and Cyril Paul who both drove the 200 hp Benz four-seater.

streamlined tail; the car which Capt. Miller rediscovered in a later decade.

Rumour was that General von Hindenburg had used it as a staff car throughout the recently-concluded war. After the Armistice, Bruno Roberts, an excitable but intelligent young bachelor whose parents had left him a fortune derived from the Waterbury Watch Company (whose products were often used in speed-traps in Edwardian days, incidentally), thought it would be fun to try his hand at Brooklands racing, the old Track having just been re-opened. He had been to see the Benz but was uncertain whether or not it would be suitable. However, he chanced to meet Mr Quince in the 'Coach and Horses' in Bruton Street. He asked Quince whether he would prepare the Benz for him, and, this being agreed, he went and bought the aged car. He had another ex-Army car, a Buick, probably bought at the Slough Trading Estate surplus sales. This was just a chassis with a box seat and had solid tyres on its back wheels. It was not an ideal towing vehicle, but it took the Benz to Roberts's garage at the Polygon at Clapham Common, where the purchase was carefully examined. It was found to have Oleo plugs, a splendid triple-grip starting handle, and a half-compression device. I am now quoting Mr Quince:

The first task was to see if the engine would start. Bruno Roberts's garage was entered through an archway, flanked on one side by a baker's shop, and on the opposite side by a butcher's. The big Benz was manhandled as far back as possible, the push-button Bosch rotary ignition switch, a huge brass-bound affair, was set to energize the two magentos, and some passing small boys were called upon to help push. The outcome was that, despite the short run available, the old Benz started, but with such an almighty backfire, said Mr Quince, that both shop windows were shattered and Roberts had to add the cost of replacing them and the price of the ruined joints of meat and cakes and pastries, to that paid for the car. (If a trumpet note brought down the walls of Jericho, I suppose an explosion

Capt. (later Sir Alastair Miller, Bt.) Miller with the 200 hp Benz four-seater which he ran at BARC meetings with astonishing results, in the hands of various drivers. In this picture, taken at the Fork, he is at the wheel, and behind the car are Ken Eggar, and C. D. Wallbank (in helmet) who also drove it. Cyril Paul actually lapped in the Benz at 115.55 mph as late as 1930, just before the ban on the older cars. Observe the typical Benz radiator snout, chain drive — and the starter motor.

The opposite side of the Sir Alastair Miller Benz, which rumour said had been Hindenburg's staff car during the 1914/18 war.

from the back of a motor car, each of whose cylinders boasted a capacity of more than five litres, could break plate-glass?!)

The engine of this pre-war Benz was discovered to be in good condition, its honeycomb radiator a work of art. But its driving chains had apparently been neglected by the German field-Army mechanics, because they had badly-worn rollers and were very rusty. However, Renold's sent two new sets free of charge and a man to advise about fitting them. They were, said Mr Quince, changed between every race meeting, the set not in use being boiled in Russian tallow and graphite. Avon supplied new 895×135 tyres with security bolts and serviced the wire wheels (there was no spare wheel), the Rudge hub nuts being tightened with a C-spanner. All was now ready for a trial at the Track, where Roberts had rented a shed. No licence disc had to be displayed in 1920 so Quince painted 'Q1' on a piece of board, tied this to the front of the Buick, put 'Q1' on the Benz, and, with no tax or other formalities, off they went.

Bruno Roberts liked to go round Brooklands in the early morning, saying that then the air was cooler, with more oxygen in it, and engines ran better. But no matter how early they went out, Col. Lindsay Lloyd, the astute Clerk-of-the-Course, would be there working a stop-watch, sometimes in his pyjamas, recalled Mr Quince. It would be unpoetic justice if this were a Waterbury, for the outcome was that the speed capabilities of the Benz were known and it never, said Quince, received a favourable handicap. It ran well enough, after its boot had been filled with lots of granite kerb stones, which were acquired surreptitiously (they were marked with broad arrows to show that convicts had made them), to improve the track holding. Even this was inadequate, so two old flywheels were added, experience proving that it was as well to wire them to the floor! The speedometer was recalibrated in mph and the speed improved after a German mechanic had told them that the second of the two Bosch magnetos should not be switched in until the Benz was doing at least 70 mph — whereupon it would surge forward. (Mr Quince said this German was advising a Mr Moir about a Mercedes-Maybach, but I think he may be confusing Kensington-Moir with Clive Gallop who may in 1920 already have been seeking information about Maybach engines for Count Zborowski.)

Harry Quince rode as passenger in the Benz in all its races, using a hand tyre pump to maintain 2 lb/sq. in. pressure in the fuel tank, as this was less messy than relying on the original exhaust-gas feed. He says that Roberts appointed a man called Buckingham, who was a lame but calm driver, to race the Benz at Brooklands. As he lived in Ebury Street, near a well-known taxi garage, also entered through an archway, the drill was to get out the Buick, go to Victoria, collect Buckingham, then drive back to Clapham to hitch on the Benz. (I cannot find any record of this person driving the Benz.) Harry Quince also says that L. G. Hornsted drove this Benz on one occasion, and that when all the oil pressure vanished he did his best to get the driver to stop, to no avail, so all the bearings were ruined. It seems that the oil-pump spindle had been hardened as well as the gears, causing it to shear. The engine was dismantled in the shed at the Track and new bearings fitted, supplied by a metal specialist in the Old Kent Road. When reassembled, the engine was too tight to hand-crank and the Buick only just managed to get it going. This may well have been before the 1920 Whitsun Meeting, because the car was posted as a non-starter because of bearing trouble.

At the August Meeting, Roberts jumped the start in the 100 mph Short Handicap and spun round after finishing. Mr Quince says this skid was put down as bad driving, but that what really happened was that one of

A typical Brooklands line-up. The Benz is No. 3, awaiting the start of the 1930 Sussex Long Handicap race.

the drivers (Olive was originally down to drive in this race) disliked security bolts, preferring that if a tyre burst it would be able to run clear rather than entangle itself in the chains. Therefore, Quince removed the bolts, but this encouraged tyres to leave the rims, which is what made the Benz slide round on this occasion. He says that ever afterwards you could see the score marks in the concrete where the wheels had scrubbed round on it. The Benz is reported to have finished slowly in the 100 mph Long Handicap that day, but this may have been one of the occasions, also recalled, when they forgot to push home the half-compression device before starting the race.

The car was not entered for the 1920 Autumn Meeting, Roberts becoming depressed when it proved unable to win. Although it was quite a good road car, Quince driving it down Piccadilly on one occasion, it was disposed of, and was soon forgotten. It appears to have been entered, with full road equipment and elaborate tool boxes on its running boards, in a Crystal Palace used-car sale in 1921, priced at £1,200. It was also, I suspect, the Benz which Hornsted entered for some Brooklands races that year, lapping at 105.97 mph before consistently non-starting. In one event it should have been driven by a Mr J. Hill, who had perhaps bought it at the aforesaid sale.

Incidentally, the improvised number plates served admirably, although my informant was finally pinched in the Buick on the day he took it to Epsom to watch the Derby. Roberts continued to buy vehicles at surplus sales, notably a batch of WD Douglas motor cycles, one of which he sold

The massive 21½-litre engine of the Benz.

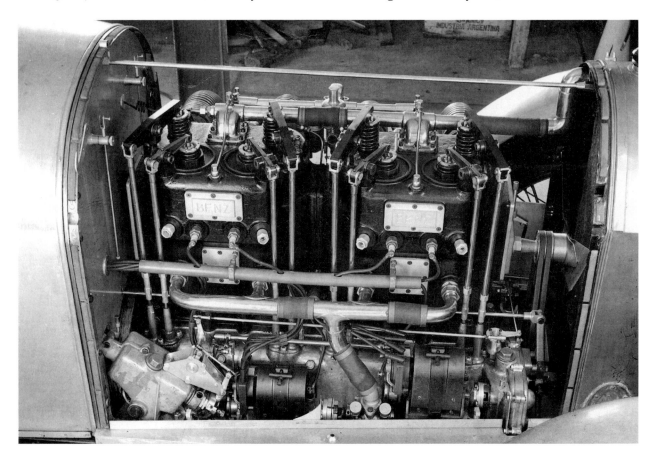

THE 200 HP BENZ FOUR-SEATER

G. K. Clowes was yet another driver of the 200 hp Benz, here seen on the Member's banking during a 1928 Surbiton Motor Club meeting at the Track. Note that both occupants are bare-headed.

to Mr Quince for £2 to replace a pre-war accumulator-ignition Hobart. There was also a sleeve-valve Argyll and a left-hand drive Darracq ambulance found abandoned in a field.

What became of the Benz's owner? He shot himself and his dog, said Mr Quince, in the house at Clapham, afterwards occupied by Nancy Spain, who died in mysterious circumstances in an aeroplane crash.

Echoing Mr Quince's story; in 1920 Bruno Roberts had entered the olive-green Benz for the August races at the revived Track following the Armistice. He had nominated G. Olive (who was later to race his EHP at Brooklands and who had a garage business on the Portsmouth Road near Guildford) to be the driver, but Roberts — who appears to have driven himself — had a miserable time. Having been towed to the starting-line, he then inadvertently jumped the start of the 100 mph Short Handicap and finally, unable to pull up properly at the top of the Finishing Straight at the end of the race, he skidded half-round and this pulled off the offside back tyre.

As stated by Mr Quince, Hornsted, who had served as a Captain during the war, was down as reserve driver in this four-seater Benz at the 1921 Summer Brooklands Meeting for the 100 mph and Lightning Short and Long Handicap races. After laps at 83.42 and 105.97 mph in the first race it failed to appear. Hornsted then brought it out for the same races at the 1921 August Bank Holiday Meeting. It was reported to be 'suffering from a mysterious internal complaint' and lapped at only 70.34 and 83.42 mph in its first engagement and was unplaced. It failed to complete a lap in the subsequent races that day, in which Mr J. Hill was down to drive it in the Lightning Short Handicap.

It seems likely that the car was bought at that Crystal Palace used-car

The Benz on parade when it was part of the Sword Collection in Scotland.

sale in April 1921, where it appears to have been the Benz priced at £1,200, with full road equipment. It also seems certain that this was the Benz which, half a dozen years later, Alastair Miller found languishing behind a pub and bought for £50, seeing it as a car well-suited to racing in the Brooklands Short Handicap races. Repainted bright red, with the customary black wheels, it made its debut in the Lightning Long Handicap at the

The impressive exhaust-pipe layout of the 200 hp Benz.

1928 Whitsun meeting, for Dudley Froy to drive. The astonished handicappers gave it 27 sec. start and it clattered round at lap speeds of 88.46,
103.33 and 99.61 mph.

Entered by Mrs A. G. Miller for G. K. Clowes to drive at a BARC
evening meeting, the old Benz opened at 74.89 mph, but retired on its next
lap. It was slower still (75.23 mph) and again retired in the second race of
the evening. Even worse, it non-started at the next of these evening frolics.

By the 1928 August meeting, Clowes made it behave to the extent of
lapping at 85.57 and 104.19 mph, and in the '100 Long' improved on this,
getting round at 89.74, 110.68 and 108.27 mph, to win from Purdy's
Thomas Special at 102.73 mph by a mere half-a-length. However, when
Dudley Watt, the pilot, drove it at the Autumn Meeting he retired in both
of his races. During the season, however, Clowes and the venerable Benz
had secured a second and a third place at a Surbiton MC meeting.

This was enough for Miller to keep the old Benz on his books for 1929,
the only attention it needed being a reconditioned radiator and petrol
tank. This proved a sage move, because the car, entrusted to C. D.
Wallbank, won the very first race of the year, the 100 mph Short
Handicap, by 150 yards at the Easter Meeting, at 97.85 mph, lapping
splendidly at 86.32 and 109.46 mph. This led to a re-handicap of 9 sec., but
Wallbank managed to finish second to Dunfee's Ballot in the '90 Long',
lapping at 91.89, 107.57 and 110.43 mph. Mrs Miller was the entrant.

The Benz non-started, perhaps deliberately, to preserve its chances, at
Whitsun. It returned for the August Bank Holiday, Miller himself driving
it into second place for his wife in the '100 Short', behind Cobb's V12
Delage, the red four-seater lapping at 93.62 and 109.94 mph. H. W. Purdy
took it out for the '100 Long', lapped at 93.44, 110.68 and 108.98 mph and
won at 104.13 mph from Kaye Don's scratch Sunbeam. Finally, this rather
astonishing Edwardian tourer was entrusted to Cyril Paul for the Autumn
Brooklands meeting and secured the same place, going on to become the
sensation of the afternoon when it won the 100 mph Long Handicap at
104 mph after lapping at 94.86, 108.98 and 109.46 mph — the pre-1914
monster giving a straight eight GP Bugatti a start of five seconds and leaving 38 seconds after the 'limit' Amilcar!

Not content with racing, the Benz, still with its touring body, broke the
International Class A 200 kilometre and 200 mile records at 72.43 and
73.15 mph, respectively. The driver on this occasion was P. Bamber. On an
earlier attempt, with Wallbank at the wheel, trouble developed and the
old Benz retired.

It was hardly surprising, after such fine running, that Miller should use
the Benz for a third season. Cyril Paul drove carefully at the opening
BARC meeting of 1930, lapping at 88.78 and 99.81 mph, retiring in the
next race. This left a comparatively good handicap intact, but laps at 90.35
and 110.68 mph at the Easter Meeting saw Paul at first unplaced. Then, in
the Sussex Long Handicap, getting going at 94.82 mph, he set up the
fastest lap to date by the four-seater Benz at 115.55 mph, and finished at
106.15 mph, to come home second behind a 4½-litre Bentley to which Paul
had given 11 sec. start.

The Benz had lost little of its astonishing pace at the Whitsun Meeting,
for Paul won the Devon Lightning Long Handicap in his ungainly tourer,
now entered by himself, at 106.91 mph; his lap speeds being 96.9, 112.93
and 112.17 mph. Mrs Miller had entered the car for the 'Gold Star'

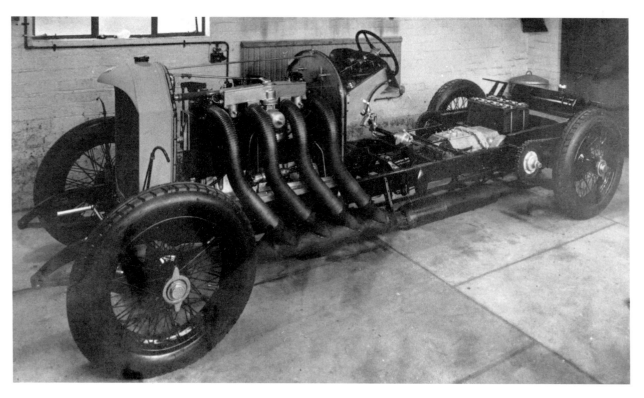

The Benz in process of being restored by Brian Morgan.

Above right *The Benz at a VSCC gathering during Eric Milner's ownership in the 1950s. The back of the body has been slightly shortened, following the Crystal Palace accident.*

Handicap, but in this Bamber non-started. However, Cyril Paul was out again for the Cornwall Long Handicap, and this time he did his standing start lap at 97.65 mph, his next lap at 115.92 mph — the old tourer's fastest ever — finishing at 110.68 mph. This won him the race, at 107.25 mph, by 5 sec. from Dunfee's Ballot. Re-handicapped 10 seconds, Paul then lapped at 94.86, 113.71 and 113.19 mph, but was unplaced in the Cornwall Lightning Long Handicap.

That these very high speeds were no fluke was shown when Paul again lapped at 97.46 and 113.19 mph in the Middlesex Senior Short Handicap at the Whitsun Meeting, being placed third; another third place falling to the Benz in the 'Senior Long', in which Paul lapped at 96.15 and 111.42 mph.

These speeds are really astonishing. Zborowski's Benz managed 106.8 mph and was easily outpaced by the Barlow and Miller cars, suggesting either that the 1909 Hemery car was getting rather long in the tooth or that somehow the Benz Company discovered ways of obtaining more power from the later Blitzen engines. I incline to the former theory, for Hornsted's car, circa 1912/13, was not appreciably quicker than Hemery's before the war. The speed of the 4-seater Benz, then at least 17 years old, is therefore quite remarkable, its 115.82 mph lap speed surpassing Barlow's fastest by 1.3 mph. Even allowing for more reliable tyres and the greater stability of a long-wheelbase chassis, it is remarkable.

The courage of those who drove such ancient giants is truly commendable; although tyres were less of a hazard by 1930, chains could break and lock the back wheels, the old engine disintegrate and fall from the chassis.

It was the vision of such horrors that caused the Brooklands authorities to ban the Benz along with other old cars from the track after 1930.

Banned from Brooklands, the old Benz vanished for a time, but when

the VSCC started events for the giant racing cars of yore (the 'Edwardians', as they were classed) John Morris of SU Carburettors rescued the car from Brooklands and brought it out in about 1936, and by 1939 was using it to good effect. When racing it at the Crystal Palace, however, he hit the bank at Stadium Dip and overturned, without much serious damage to either driver or car. The body of the Benz, however, had to

On the road. The big Benz tourer after its extensive rebuild by Eric Milner.

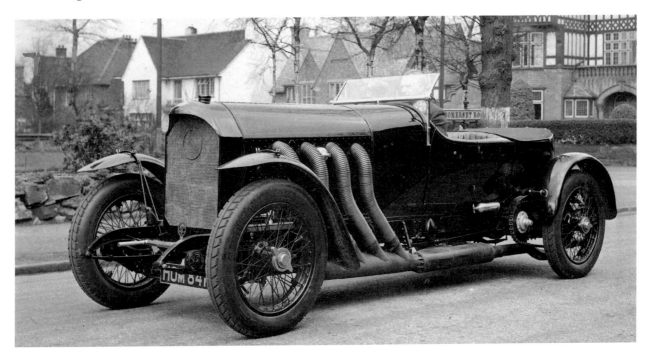

*The long-lived 1912
Benz as it appears at
the time of writing —
an exhibit in the City
Museum and Art
Gallery in
Birmingham, who
supplied the
photograph.*

be somewhat rebuilt, resulting in the tonneau being shortened and the
two back doors being scrapped, although it remained a handsome motor
car, and a formidable one, capable of climbing Shelsley-Walsh in 50 seconds. Eric Milner, a Director of Benton & Stone, then took the car in hand
and effected a meticulous restoration. He had seen Hornsted race the Big
Benz at the Track before the war and was delighted to persuade John to
part with it, around 1946/7. He discovered that only one pair of original
cylinders remained, so set about having patterns and core boxes made for
two new pairs, at a cost of £250 in the 1950s, plus a 'tenner' to have them
dimensionally checked. New 7-in. long exhaust rockers, push-rods and
bronze tapper-guides were made, and a new induction pipe and carburettor were necessary as the original had been lost. After many failures, with
the huge engine running terribly roughly, Milner made a big Zenith-type
carburettor himself, to replace the two semi-downdraught $2\frac{1}{2}$ in. SUs that
had stuck in uncharacteristic fashion through the bonnet side.

Not only that, but he made a new radiator, as the matrix had been
smashed on the original one. No one could formulate the Benz square
tubes, so his tube mill was set about producing 7,500 complicated tubes,
0.005 in. thick and 4 in. long by a quarter square, with more tubes to hold
them, taking months of maddening work. The 2 ft.-diameter cone clutch
was heavy and fierce, so servo assistance was added, and the gearbox casing had split when Morris had used the Benz for sand racing. Brian
Morgan, master of old car rebuilding, came to the rescue after 'Chitty-
Bang-Bang' had been bought from the Conan Doyle brothers (see *Aero-
Engined Cars at Brooklands* Haynes/Foulis, 1992) and scrapped, after the
unrealized hope that its gearbox could be adapted. Brian Morgan made a
new casing, and new gears were required, as the split in the Benz casing

had been caused by some teeth coming off the big first-gear pinion and getting between the constant-mesh gears, forcing them apart and thus destroying the casing.

This led to a misunderstanding when I told Owen Wyn-Owen that the Higham Special 'Babs', which he had disinterred from Pendine and ably restored, had always had a 200 hp Benz gearbox. He said he had looked under the ex-Milner Benz in the Birmingham Museum and the casing was different. This surprised me, as I had assumed that all the gearboxes for the Blitzen Benz, the 'Jumbo' Blitzens and the 'touring' long-wheelbase versions were the same. The answer became clear when, in 1987, Brian told me of the modification he had to make to the box in the ex-Miller car.

Eric Milner fitted Girling back-wheel brakes, because with the Benz brakes 'you had to drive about two villages ahead', and as he was getting too old to crank a 21½-litre engine, he installed a 24-volt starter with a large reduction gear, located out of sight. In 1951 he toured France in the Benz and enjoyed what a friend described as 'just like wearing seven league boots'. The steering was excellent, and the top gear ratio then was 1.4-to-1, with 35x6 tyres, equal to 127 mph should the peak engine speed of 1,450 rpm be possible. Milner also used the Benz for sprint competitions, and at a VSCC event at Madresfield in 1949 he clocked a remarkable 12.2 seconds in the acceleration test, the Benz beaten only by a Ford V8-engined Frazer Nash and a Hudson Special.

Brian Morgan himself then took over the Benz and eventually sold it to someone who was unfortunately killed in a motor cycle accident. This new owner had already lent the car to the Birmingham Museum of Science and Industry and his family have allowed it to remain as an exhibit there.

13. The 10½-litre V12 Delage

The 10½-litre V12 Delage, raced by many skilled drivers over a considerable period with notable success, so that it became one of the outstanding Brooklands giants, seen at speed on the Members' banking.

The Delage Company had been successful in hill-climbs with a 5.1-litre six-cylinder car built specially for the purpose and, thus encouraged, built a bigger sprint car for the 1923 Gaillon hill-climb.

News of this car was released in England in the autumn, and René Thomas was announced as the driver appointed to drive it, the car being described as of 350 hp.

The engine had two banks of six separate cylinders, each of 90×140 mm, giving a total swept volume of 10,688 cc. Vertical offset overhead valves, two per cylinder, were operated by a single camshaft carrying the 24 cams. The push-rods were on the inside of the 'V' formed by the cylinders, and tubular pillars provided pivots for the rockers. Ignition was by two magnetos placed side-by-side low down on the front of the crankcase; a fan assisted cooling of the big radiator, which was protected by a grille, and each cylinder bank had its own water intake. Dry-sump lubrication was used. The disc-web crank-bearings had an outside diameter of 90

The first racing driver to tame the old LSR Delage in this country was John Cobb in 1929, who by 1933 had set a Class A lap record with it of 133.38 mph. He was eventually to set the all-time Brooklands lap record to 143.44 mph in 1935 with the aero-engined Napier-Railton.

mm; the crankpin diameter was 64 mm. The con-rods were tubular, with four-bolt big-ends and three fins on each bearing cap. The rods were mounted side-by-side on each journal. The camshaft ran in seven ball-races and had a cam for actuating the air-feed pump at the rear. The alloy pistons each carried five rings, one in the skirt base, and 1¹/₈-in. floating gudgeon-pins were used. The rev limit was 3,200 rpm.

The chassis frame was of conventional channel-section and looked somewhat inadequate for such a powerful car. The side-members were braced by only four cross-members, these consisting of a drilled I-section member at the front and another at the rear, and two small-diameter tubular members extended to constitute hangers for the road springs. The engine, however, was relied on to stiffen things up, the alloy crankcase, in itself a magnificent piece of foundry work, being extended out to the chassis and attached thereto at four points on each side. The clutch was a multi-plate, devoid of a clutch stop. Suspension was by ¹/₂-elliptic springs, shackled at their rear ends, the back axle being underslung. The front axle was of I-section. Two pairs of triple Hartford friction shock-absorbers were fitted at the rear, and there was a triple Hartford on each side of each front spring. The fuel tank was quite small, although it was extended rearwards at some stage in the car's career. It occupied the tail, being held on at one point on each side and braced by a metal strap to the rear cross-member. The wheelbase measured 9 ft. 3 in., the front track 4 ft. 9 in., the rear track 4 ft. 7¹/₂ in., and the front wheels were inclined, to give centre-point steering.

The body was a single-seater, although at one period a passenger's seat was fitted, this being possible because the steering wheel was located towards the offside of the car, a fairing over the near side of the cockpit being fitted normally. The control levers were typically Delage, a grab-handle for the passenger and a pressure-pump (on the inside of the scuttle on the left) were fitted, and the facia carried a Parisian Jaeger rev-counter reading to 6,000 rpm, two tumbler switches, two Aric thermometers, a Delage pressure-gauge and an oil-gauge. The engine crankcase, providing as it did a housing for the huge central crankshaft bearing and also acting as a stiffener for the chassis, had a rather trying time, and after a few years creeping cracks appeared, to the consternation of the Brooklands scrutineers. At the Track 33x5.35 in. tyres were fitted.

Although a sprint car, the Delage had front brakes from its inception, these having Perrot-type actuation. It came to this country with a choice of seven rear axle ratios, ranging from 3.36-to-1 to 1.95-to-1, a 2.18-to-1 ratio being normally employed at Brooklands. Thomson & Taylor raised the compression ratio to 7-to-1 when the car arrived in this country so that it then possessed an excellent power/weight ratio. It was well streamlined, the single-seater mottled-aluminium body having a tapering tail, and the radiator at that time being covered by the conventional cowl, while the dumb-irons were faired in. Six exhaust pipes emerged from the bonnet on each side. The early system of carburation consisted of two long copper manifolds, each fed by a huge double-choke updraught Zenith carburettor. This later gave way to four Zenith downdraughts, each feeding three cylinders.

Although the Delage Company only used this handsome giant for a few years, it built up useful prestige for them. Thomas had broken the record at Gaillon (held at the time of the 1923 Paris Salon, and for which the big Delage was initially prepared) at a speed of 72.6 mph, and had made second fastest time in the six-cylinder Delage. In 1925 the 10½-litre V12 Delage raised this record to 75.57 mph. No doubt the big Delage took other hill-climb honours, although it seems that its bulk hampered it on most courses, which is why the major hill-climb honours seem to have been gained by the smaller six-cylinder car, which encouraged Delage to build another, of similar dimensions, with a 5.9-litre twin-overhead-camshaft engine, for the 1925 season.

However, they had other work for the 12-cylinder car. At Arpajon in July 1924 René Thomas used the Delage to break the World Land Speed Record, with a speed of 143.26 mph over this narrow public-road kilometre, and 143.312 mph over the mile, the latter speed improving on the former record — held since 1922 by K. Lee Guinness in the 18.3-litre V12 Sunbeam over the Brooklands kilometre — by 9.56 mph. As a matter of fact, Ernest Eldridge, in his ancient 21-litre aeroplane-engined Fiat, had gone a few miles an hour faster than René Thomas, but the latter put in his historic protest about the Fiat having no reverse gear, and the Delage was given the record and proudly displayed in the Delage showrooms in the Champs-Elysées in Paris, labelled as 'The Fastest Car in the World'. Its fame was short-lived, for a few days later Eldridge, equipped with a means of reversing, raised the record to 146.01 mph. At the time, Thomas's protest was regarded in England as very unsporting, but it must be remembered that he was a professional driver in the employ of the Delage Company. The French driver's protest caused the Welsh racing driver, J. G. Parry Thomas, to write to the papers to emphasize that it was René Thomas, not he, who had acted thus, saying that surely racing drivers could still be sportsmen? He challenged the Frenchman to a four-lap duel at Brooklands and a similar race at the new Montlhéry Autodrome near Paris — the single-seater Delage against his two-seater 7.2-litre Leyland-Thomas. Parry Thomas promised not to dig up any obsolete (and somewhat confused) rules if he lost! This duel never happened, but at Montlhéry in 1925 Albert Divo did beat Parry Thomas, in a match race;

the big Delage setting a new lap-record of 136.53 mph (41.8 seconds), beating Parry Thomas's previous lap-record with the Leyland-Thomas, of 135.07 mph.

Probably because of their desire to take the World Land Speed Record, Delage did not run the car at the newly-opened Montlhéry track during 1924, although there was a suitable match race there for it in October. However, in June 1925 Albert Divo brought the Delage to Montlhéry for a match race against the same three cars which had fought it out in 1924, namely Parry Thomas's Leyland-Thomas, Eldridge's enormous Fiat, which had vanquished the Delage at Arpajon, and a Borgenschutz Special with a 180 hp V8 Hispano-Suiza aero-engine. The race was over 9.3 miles, and the Delage averaged 125.5 mph, setting that new Montlhéry lap-record of 136.53 mph, and beating the Leyland-Thomas and Fiat.

At the end of the year Robert Benoist brought the Delage out and broke the flying-start 5-mile and 5-kilometre records, and the 10-kilometre record, averaging 133 mph for the five miles. These records had stood previously to the credit of Parry Thomas's 8-litre Leyland-Thomas. After this the Delage Company became involved with its 2-litre V12 Grand Prix cars and put the three sprint cars aside.

John Cobb, who had always liked racing the 'heavy metal' at Brooklands, was finding his 1911 10-litre chain-drive Fiat rather worn in the bores, and when Capt. (later Sir) Alastair Miller went out to Paris in February 1928 to look at the two six-cylinder Delage sprint cars, which were for sale, he also inspected the V12 Delage on behalf of Thomson & Taylor (Brooklands) Ltd, who were negotiating on Cobb's behalf. Miller bought both the six-cylinder cars, calling them Delage I and Delage II.

Presumably Miller reported favourably about the V12 car, because Thomson & Taylor acquired it and prepared it for Cobb in time for the 1929 Brooklands season. It was stabled at T & T's Brooklands establishment and entered by them for Cobb to drive; although he was the car's owner, the entrant appeared as K. J. Thomson. The car was bought with many spares, including a selection of seven back-axle ratios, ranging from 3.36-to-1 to 1.95-to-1. In preparation for racing at the track T & T raised the compression-ratio to 7-to-1 (better fuels being available than when the Delage first raced) and put in the 2.18-to-1 axle ratio. The car still had its radiator cowl and mottled aluminium bodywork, but the front dumb-irons were now completely faired-in, and an aero screen was fitted to the scuttle. The chassis was blue, the wheels black.

There is some confusion as to whether a new single-seater body was fitted at this time, or whether the old two-seater body had been modified, but if the former, the width was much greater than most of the single-seaters evolved for Brooklands. However, the exhaust-pipes, emerging coyly at the scuttle, were replaced by six separate stub pipes coming out on each side of the bonnet leading into single pipes, in turn leading to the Brooklands silencers. Uncertainty also exists about the carburation developments. Originally four Zeniths were said to supply the mixture, but later two long copper inlet manifolds were used, each one fed by a huge double-choke updraught Zenith. Later again this was changed to four downdraught Zenith carburetters, each one feeding three cylinders.

The Delage was entered for the 1929 BARC meeting and, although this was Cobb's first race in her, and he was having trouble changing gear because the clutch would not free properly, he contrived to finish third

The start of a race at the BRDC British Empire Trophy Meeting with Cobb in the big Delage (No. 47) and the contrasting 1½-litre straight-eight Delage on the extreme left of the line-up.

behind Wallbank in the 21½-litre Benz four-seater and E. L. Bouts in his 5-litre Indianapolis Sunbeam. Cobb had started from scratch, such was his reputation and that of the Delage, giving these competitors, respectively, a start of 43 sec. and 32 sec. in 6½ miles. He lapped at 107.34 and 123.28 mph.

Cobb came out again for the Founders' Gold Cup Lightning Short Handicap, being on scratch with Kaye Don's supercharged 4-litre V12 Sunbeam. He was unplaced, but kept ahead of Don and lapped at 100.61 and 126.09 mph. Cobb decided this was sufficient for a first attempt and scratched from the Lightning Long Handicap. At the 1929 Whitsun BARC meeting Cobb started from scratch in the Gold Vase 100 mph Short Handicap, completing his standing start lap at 108.51 mph and doing his flying lap at 125.77 mph, which gave the Delage a third place behind Don's supercharged 2-litre Sunbeam, which had 7 sec. start, and Dunfee's sister car, which left at the same time. Cobb found no room to pass these scorching Sunbeams. Out again in the 'Lightning Long', Cobb really got going, doing his standing start lap at 112.93 mph (which would have been a new record if Don hadn't done 115.29 mph in the Sunbeam 'Tiger') and his flying laps at 122.37 and 132.11 mph, which won him the race at 121.81 mph.

The Delage continued in winning form at the 1929 BARC August Bank Holiday Meeting. On its usual scratch position in the 100 mph Short Handicap, it lapped at 112.42 mph, having entered the Railway Straight level with the old Benz and pulled out 0.8 sec. on it as they crossed the finishing line. Cobb tried hard in the Lightning Short Handicap, but nearly lost control near the aeroplane sheds while trying to pass Froy's Delage I, which was travelling very high up the Byfleet banking. The big Delage raised a cloud of dust as a wheel nearly went over the edge, but Cobb held her. However, he was obliged to lift off and Froy won by 2.2 sec.,

Cobb second. The V12 car's lap speeds were 108.03 and 124.51 mph.

Undaunted, Cobb was out again for the 'Lightning Long' (lap speeds: 97.85, 114.23 and 112.68 mph) the car being off form, or else Cobb was hoping to improve his future handicap. The former is the more likely explanation, as the Delage was withdrawn from the Gold Star 25-mile Handicap.

At the Autumn Brooklands Meeting, held on 21 September, Cobb, as ever on scratch, was unplaced in the '100 Short' in spite of lapping at 108.98 and 123.58 mph, and then, in a tricky wind, won the 'Lightning Short' at 112.43 mph, 80 yards ahead of Jack Dunfee in the 3-litre straight-eight Ballot, the Delage lapping at 108.27 mph and 118.58 mph; so it was running well within itself. Coming out for the last race of the day, Cobb carried a re-handicap of over 5 sec. but still contrived to take second place, behind Dufee's 2-litre Sunbeam, after lapping at 106.65, 124.82 and 122.67 mph, although the engine was misfiring. This was a first season to be proud of indeed!

At this autumn meeting the old Delage ran with its radiator cowl removed, to display its big radiator. In fact, this was a new radiator made for T & T by Serck, with a header tank behind it, the original probably being regarded as inadequate for Brooklands racing. In England the car had run without the fairings over the rear dumb-irons and cross-member, although when an artist working for *The Autocar* illustrated the car at about this time he showed the rear ends of the chassis side-members as terminating in knife-edges, either being misled by the original fairings or intending to depict these.

Cobb regarded the BRDC 500-mile Race as too strenuous for the old Delage and drove Jack Dunfee's V12 4-litre Sunbeam in this race. But earlier in the year, in April, he had used the Delage for record-breaking, at well over 128 mph, and had taken the Class A 50-kilometre and mile and

Battle of the Giants! The commencement of the BRDC British Empire Trophy Race of 1932. It was an extremely close-run thing between Capt. G. E. T. Eyston in the 8-litre Panhard-Levassor and Cobb in the Delage, but after a protest by Eyston had been upheld, then rescinded, the race was awarded to Cobb, who had averaged 126.363 mph. Cobb was No. 47, Eyston No. 44, and No. 46 is Sir Henry Birkin's blower 4 ½-litre single-seater Bentley.

John Cobb, who won the very close-fought and high-speed 1932 British Empire Trophy Race in the big Delage, and Capt. George Eyston, OBE, MC, in the 8-litre Panhard-Levassor which lost by 1/5th second at the end of the 100 miles.

100-mile records to over 119 mph. Then, in September, the racing season over for the Delage, Cobb took the very difficult one-hour Class A record, at Brooklands, to 112.18 mph, taking also the 100-mile record on the way and finally, assisted by Cyril Paul, Cobb got the Class A 200-kilometre and 200-mile records, at 105.97 and 107.56 mph.

It is interesting to speculate on why John Cobb attacked records. Did he do so because he was proud of his car and wanted it to capture every honour open to it or, rich fur-broker though he was, did he use the bonus fees such successful attempts earned to reduce the expense of letting Thomson & Taylor Ltd prepare the Delage for him? Whatever the incentive, Cobb broke more records with the car during the 1930 season.

A brief illness kept Cobb away from the BARC Easter Meeting although K. J. Thomson had entered the Delage for one race. All was well at Whitsun, when Cobb, now starting 10 sec. before Don's lap-record Sunbeam 'Tiger', won the Devon Lightning Short Handicap at 116.88 mph, lapping at 110.19 and 125.14 mph.

Back on scratch with Sir Henry ('Tim') Birkin's supercharged single-seater 4½-litre Bentley (which, however, non-started) at the August Brooklands Meeting, Cobb was awarded the 'Lightning Short' race (after Craig's Bugatti, which finished first, had been disqualified), his average speed 121.08 mph, and lap speeds 113.97 and 126.09 mph. Cobb then won the Lightning Long Handicap, the old car getting round at 113.19 mph on its first lap and pulling out 130.04 and 124.82 mph on its two flying laps, an average of 121.18 mph. The Autumn races saw Cobb come home second behind Munday's 'limit' 30/98 Vauxhall in the Senior Short Handicap, in which the Delage started from scratch and lapped at 110.68 and 125.45 mph. By now Cobb had the handling of this difficult giant absolutely buttoned up, and he drove it comparatively steadily. Another second place fell to him in the Senior Long Handicap, which was won by Daybell's 'limit' 30/98 Vauxhall, the Delage being on scratch but not re-handicapped, and lapping at 108.27, 125.45 and 123.89 mph.

The 1931 season opened successfully for the Delage, Cobb winning the Lincoln Lightning Long Handicap at the Opening Brooklands meeting in March at 111.37 mph, by 1.8 sec. from Bouts's Indianapolis Sunbeam, the winner's lap speeds being 112.17 and 114.23 mph. Admittedly there were only four starters, but Cobb had to give Bouts 35 seconds. This earned Cobb a re-handicap of 15 seconds from his original scratch start in the equivalent Long Handicap, but he increased speed to 110.68, 127.7 and 125.45 mph, this time finishing second to Bouts, 11.6 sec. in arrears, the old Sunbeam having this time been flagged away 6.2 sec before the French car.

At Easter, Cobb was unplaced in the Lightning Short Handicap, although lapping at 113.71 and at 129.72 mph from 'owes 3 sec.', W. B. Scott's 1^1/$_2$-litre Delage being third behind a Bugatti and a Bentley. However, the big Delage came into the picture again in the Founders' Gold Cup Race, in which it was second, 6.4 sec behind Pollack's Bugatti, Cobb lapping at exactly the same speed as before on his standing lap and at 128.03 and 130.72 mph on his flying laps.

The 1923 Delage had already put up an unrivalled record of successful racing at Brooklands, and at Whitsun Cobb proceeded, in the One Lap Sprint Handicap, to equal Don's record standing lap of 115.29 mph, finishing second once again to Munday's Vauxhall.

Unfortunately, disaster was close at hand. Coming out for the 20-mile 'Gold Star' Handicap in which he had 5 sec. start from Sir Henry Birkin, Bt., in the Hon. Dorothy Paget's blower-4 ^{1}/$_2$ Bentley single-seater, which was to become a serious rival to the older Delage, Cobb came in second, 2.8 sec. behind Earl Howe's 1^1/$_2$-litre Delage. But, inadvertently, he drove eight laps instead of the required seven, and on this unnecessary additional lap a con-rod came out through the side of the crankcase. The Delage had been going fast, its standing lap being completed at 113.97 mph and its seventh lap, the fastest in the race, at 132.8 mph, using a lower axle ratio than before.

Fortunately Thomson & Taylor had another crankcase among the spares bought with the car, so its remarkable career was hardly interrupted. Indeed it was out again at the BARC August Meeting of 1931, now with four downdraught Zenith carburettors, one per three cylinders, although it did not show its previous form, running unplaced in two races — its best lap-speed only 128.03 mph. Perhaps this was because it had only just been run-in before racing started. At the Autumn Meeting, which concluded the 1932 Brooklands season, Cobb was slower and unplaced in his first race, but was back on form in the Senior Long Handicap, in which he lapped at 110.68, 129.36 and 130.38 mph to finish second to Widengren's OM.

For the 1932 season, in spite of the increasing competition from Birkin's

Bentley, Cobb decided to continue racing the Delage. Old cars were by now suspect at Brooklands, and the authorities, having had a report from the scrutineers of creeping cracks in the crankcase of the Delage, restricted it to races of less than 150 miles, with no corners.

This did not deter Cobb, who was primarily an outer-circuit driver, and he entered the great aluminium and blue car for the Easter BARC Meeting. Starting from scratch with the red Birkin Bentley in the Norfolk Lightning Short Handicap, the Delage did its opening lap at 110.19 mph, compared to the Bentley's 104.41 mph and, although the supercharged car opened up to 134.24 mph on its flying laps, to Cobb's 128.36 mph, acceleration gained the day and the Delage won, at 119.24 mph, by a mere fifth of a second. These two very fast cars met again in the 'Lightning Long', the Delage this time being given a start of 3 sec., and, able to get into its stride over three laps, the Bentley beat Cobb, catching the Delage halfway round the Byfleet banking on the last lap. The Delage lapped at 111.42, 122.97 and 124.20 mph.

The BRDC British Empire Trophy Meeting at Brooklands on 30 April saw a hard-fought battle amongst the 'heavy metal'. First there were heats, and in his Cobb was happy to come in third, at 119.11 mph behind Eyston's single-seater 8-litre Panhard-Levassor and Jack Dunfee's 6½-litre Bentley. In the final, over 100-miles, Cobb decided to open up when within 16 miles of the finish, thus sparing the old Delage as much as possible. Consequently, he led away from the start but eased up after three laps, holding third place behind Birkin's Bentley and Eyston's Panhard. Then, perhaps as Cobb had surmised, the Bentley began to pop and bang and, after it had stopped, Eyston took the lead, pursued relentlessly by the other French car. On the 26th lap, as Eyston eased back slightly, fearful of tyre trouble, Cobb went by, on the inside going into the Railway Straight.

The task of holding these big cars at over 120 mph was very tiring but a titanic duel ensued. Eyston opened up immediately on being overtaken, but nowhere could he get past the Delage. Cobb found his plan frustrated and opened full-out 30 miles from the finish, averaging 128.65 mph for the second half of this now historic race. Eyston tried to pass inside at the Fork but to no avail. The Delage was declared the winner, at 126.363 mph. The Panhard came in right behind it (official race speed: 126.354 mph) and threw a tyre tread as proof that Eyston's earlier anxiety was prudence, not cowardice. Eyston protested he had been baulked, and after a 2½-hour conference he was awarded the race, by ⅕ sec. Cobb appealed. His appeal was upheld. He won £100 but Eyston took only £10 less in prize money, although he paid for a dinner to Cobb to show there were no ill-feelings over his motor racing legal hearing. (See also Appendix 3.)

At Whitsun the 10½-litre Delage was out again, but a lap at 101.23 mph was insufficient to get it a place in the Sprint Handicap. On scratch with Birkin in the Senior Short Handicap, Cobb had a fine battle with the Bentley, beating it to third place by inches, after lapping at 106.88 and 126.09 mph.

For the 20-mile 'Gold Star' Handicap, Birkin, and Howe's 4.9-litre Bugatti, had to give 8 sec. start to the Delage, which had never gone better. Cobb came in third, behind Munday's Vauxhall and Bouts's GP Sunbeam, and his fourth lap, at 133.16 mph, broke his own Class A lap-record by a handsome margin. He averaged 130.5 mph.

At the JCC Guy's Gala Meeting, when the Graf Zeppelin flew over

Brooklands, the Delage again raised the Class A lap-record, to 133.88 mph; although, badly baulked by slower cars, Cobb couldn't catch Ashby's Riley in the Duke of York's six-lap race. Imagine trying to ease up from over 130 mph in the virtually brakeless Delage when slower stuff got in your path!

For the 1932 August BARC Meeting, Cobb drove the single-seater Talbot 105 for Arthur Fox, but he also had the Delage out for the Lightning Short Handicap, in which laps at 111.92 mph and 132.8 mph failed to secure him a place. Later that afternoon the Delage appeared in a three-lap Invitation Race against Birkin's blower-4¹/₂ Bentley, for 100 sovs. It was a stirring affair, entirely typical of outer-circuit Brooklands. Birkin just managed to pull it off, by ¹/₅ sec., or perhaps 25 yards! To do so the Bentley lapped at 137.58 mph, or only 0.28 mph below the lap record speed. The Delage lapped at 112.17, 132.46 and 133.16 mph, being caught only on the line.

Perhaps Cobb was finding the faithful old car a bit frail, because he didn't drive it again that day. He did have his customary two races in the Delage at the Autumn Meeting, lapping at 111.17 and 131.76 mph in the first, at 111.67 and 131.76 mph in the second, but was unplaced in this, his last appearance in a car which had served him so supremely well.

By 1933, outer-circuit races were fewer, to accommodate the Mountain-circuit handicaps, and Cobb must have been anxious to win those that were still held. Conscious that Birkin's Bentley held the Brooklands lap record at 137.96 mph, whereas his Delage had not bettered 133.88 mph,

The next driver to race the Delage was the handsome blond-haired barrister Oliver Bertram, seen here returning to the Paddock after winning the 1935 Whitsun Lightning Short Handicap. The Delage (No. 1) was entered by photographer Louis Klementaski. The Delage is followed by Richard Marker's 6¹/₂-litre Bentley.

Oliver Bertram with a group of his admiring friends.

Cobb got Thomson & Taylor to build him the 24-litre Napier Railton, the story of which is told in my book *Aero-Engined Racing Cars at Brooklands* (Foulis/Haynes, 1992).

However, the Brooklands career of the venerable V12 Delage was by no means finished. That debonair, blond young barrister, Oliver Bertram, acquired it for £400 and got Robin Jackson to service it in the Little Paddock at Brooklands. Repainted blue, with black wheels, and the radiator vented to a point alongside the cockpit, the old car looked much as before. A rather nice touch was that Cobb had displayed the new BARC car badge on the Delage, and Oliver Bertram continued to do this when he was racing the car. Starting carefully, by lapping at 91.95 mph for the Sprint race at the 1933 Opening Meeting, Bertram, still on the scratch mark, came home second in his second race in the car, $^3/_5$ sec. behind Baker's 'limit' Minerva, in the Sprint Handicap, lapping at 92.35 mph. He repeated this performance in the next race of this sort, at exactly the same speed, being second to Freddie Dixon's Riley by 1.8 sec.

The full circuit was available again at Easter, and Bertram took the Delage round it at 102.69 and 119.15 mph in his first race, and at 103.11, 120.88 and 121.77 mph in his second, but was unplaced. At Whitsun, however, he drove the car into second place in the 20-mile 'Gold Star' Handicap, 10.2 sec. behind Brackenbury's winning Bugatti, his standing lap having been accomplished at 93.97 mph and his best lap at 128.36 mph. At the Inter-Club Meeting in July, Bertram lapped at 105.29 and 120.88 mph in the first race and, coming out for the '100 Long', took second place behind Miss Schwedler's Alvis, lapping at 105.29, 121.18, and 122.07 mph. It was a busy day for Bertram, because he was out again for the five-lap Handicap, but lap speeds of 104.41, 122.37, 121.47, 120.88 and 122.07 mph found him outside the place positions. His consistent lap times are significant, however. He was lucky to be able to run, because previously, at the BRDC British Empire Trophy Meeting, the Delage had broken its crown wheel during the big race.

Success came to the new combination in August, when Bertram won the Byfleet Senior Short Handicap, admittedly by the narrow margin of ²/₅ sec., from Dixon's Riley 9, at 118.05 mph, lapping at 107.1 and 127.7 mph. This led to a 3 sec. re-handicap in the 'Lightning Short' but the Delage was third, behind Cobb's new Napier-Railton and Kaye Don's 4.9-litre Bugatti, its lap speeds up to 110.68 and 129.03 mph.

The Delage was absent from the 1933 Autumn Meeting. For the 1934 season the Brooklands authorities required a new front axle (made by Robin Jackson) to be fitted to the old Delage, although as this wasn't ready, it was permitted to run at the Opening Meeting with the existing axle. In any case, because of winter repairs, the outer circuit wasn't available, so the car was only committed to the First Walton half-mile Scratch Race, which it won, at 89.11 mph, comfortably ahead of Oats's Maserati. It then disposed of Fotheringham's Bugatti to win the Third Walton Half-mile Scratch Race, although by only ¹/₅ sec.

Over to the full circuit at Easter, Bertram and the Delage were again in winning form. They just snatched the Esher Lightning Short Handicap, by ¹/₅ sec from Cobb's 2.3-litre straight-eight Alfa-Romeo (a small car for

Bertram at speed along the half-mile Railway Straight in the Delage. No. 1 denotes that it started from the scratch mark, as it usually did, and the colours are those of the short-lived Junior Racing Drivers' Club.

Cobb!), lapping at 111.67 and 131.41 mph, to average 121.7 mph. Bertram came out in the four-lap Brooklands Championship Race, but although he lapped at 111.42, 132.8, 133.88 and 133.16 mph, he had to give the best to Cobb's Napier-Railton and Don's big supercharged Bugatti, this being a scratch contest.

It is particularly interesting that in his next race, the 'Esher Lightning Long', Bertram again put in a best lap at 133.88 mph — the Delage seemed to have reached its limit, but was going magnificently for an 11-year-old car. In fact, it was second in this race to Fotheringham's Bugatti, doing its other laps at 131.19 and 132.8 mph — note again the consistency of the flying laps. Bertram's standing-start lap at over 113 mph was very creditable; Cobb had done better but on a slightly lower axle ratio.

Somewhat slower, at 111.67, 128.69 and 131.06 mph, Bertram was unplaced in his first race at the Autumn Meeting, driving in place of Mrs Elsie Wisdom, who had been nominated. This availed him nothing. Brian Twist of *The Autocar* took the car through the Senior Long Handicap for a journalistic stunt, lapping at 102.27, 124.2 and 123.28 mph. He, too, was unplaced. The car was using the 2.18-to-1 axle ratio, which gave a speed of 115 mph at 2,500 rpm and 138 mph at 3,000 rpm.

Apart from using it at Brooklands, Bertram took the car to Southport sands and did 122.9 mph in a kilometre race, made ftd at the Varsity Speed Trials, twice made second-ftd at Brighton, and climbed Shelsley-Walsh in 52 sec. on a wet day. He also took it to Syston Park in 1935 and, after some gearbox problems in practice, made fastest time in the speed trials there, in 28.86 seconds, using twin rear wheels. In fact, soon after acquiring the Delage, Bertram had taken it to Gospall Park for the 1933 Inter-Varsity Speed Trials, in order to learn how to drive his new possession (to obtain which he had sold a Phantom I Rolls-Royce). On this first outing Bertram set fastest time of the day. He also competed at the Lewes speed trials.

But, clearly, for outer-circuit work near the lap record bracket, a lap-speed in the region of 140 mph had become necessary, and as the 8-litre Bentley Barnato-Hassan was being built for Bertram, he was anxious to sell the Delage.

He found a buyer in Louis Klemantaski, the studio and motor racing photographer who had founded the Junior Racing Drivers' Club. He saw in the big Delage a means of introducing JRDC members to a taste of really high speed. The car was repainted black, lined in the Club colours and the body altered to a token two-seater, which necessitated scrapping the rounded tail for one of more pointed Grand Prix shape.

While he was waiting for his Barnato-Hassan, Bertram drove the Delage for Klemantaski, lapping at 107.34 mph at the Opening BARC Meeting of 1935 without being in the picture. Capt. Woolf Barnato entered the Barnato-Hassan for Bertram at the Easter Meeting, so Klemantaski got Mrs Kay Petre to drive the Delage for him. This entailed altering seat and pedals to accommodate the slight form of this very brave and skilled lady

The big Delage in sprint mode, driven by Bertram at Syston Park. Note its twin back wheels.

Above *After some tuition from Bertram, little Mrs Kay Petre excelled with the Delage, finally lapping in it at 134.75 mph. She is seen here (right) with another fine lady driver, Mrs Elsie ('Bill') Wisdom.*

Above right *The very courageous Kay Petre in the cockpit of the giant Delage, the seat and pedals of which had to be adapted to her petite stature.*

driver. Apparently, to get her accustomed to the car, Oliver Bertram drove Kay round the Track at laps of 130 mph, Kay sitting unperturbable beside him. In the end, of course, she lapped faster than Cobb had in the car, and John Cobb, Oliver Bertram and Kay Petre all got their 130 mph Brooklands badges with the ageing Delage. It is a compliment to her that in her first race in the Delage she was put on scratch with Bertram in his new car! Kay lapped at 102.9 and 127.38 mph. Bertram won, she was unplaced. Bertram then went back to the Delage for the next race, the Easter Lightning Short Handicap, lapped at 113.97 and 135.34 mph (his fastest lap — but then the car was no longer his own!) and won by 6.8 sec. from Marker's Bentley-Jackson, at 124.36 mph.

(There is a delightful story told of the JRDC's association with the Delage. It concerns a young City gentleman, who came down to Brooklands one evening, a prospective member of this new club. He handed bowler hat and neatly-rolled umbrella to a bystander, got into the driving seat of the car, and proceeded to lap very fast indeed. As he came in, the onlookers gathered round, impressed by his prowess, anxious to hear his comments. Retrieving his City accoutrements, he said that he did not find anything sufficiently exciting about driving on the track to induce him to take up motor racing, and went on his way. The story is Rivers-Fletcher's, who swears it is true! It had a parallel when my youngest daughter, taken up in a glider for a trial flight, stepped out and remarked that she had found the experience boring in the extreme.)

Bertram had made an attempt on the lap-record at the Whitsun Meeting, in the Barnato-Hassan, so the Delage was rather a back number for him. Mrs Kay Petre drove it for the JRDC at the August Meeting. She was clearly getting proficient in the big car, lapping at 95.41 and 130.72 mph in her first race and then taking part in a two-lap Match Race for 50 sovs., against Gwenda Stewart's supercharged 1.6-litre fwd Derby. Kay already held the ladies' Lap Record with the Delage, at 129.58 mph, when this race was arranged, but Gwenda had been round Montlhéry at 147.8 mph. The evening before the race Kay had replied, with a lap at 134.75. In the event the Derby burst its silencer after lapping at 133.67 mph, whereas the Delage, running first — the scandalized officials refused to let the ladies actually race — did 129.03 mph, then 134.24 mph, but it was not on form and the clutch was slipping, so that Bertram, intending to drive it in the August Long Handicap, had to withdraw. Before she returned to France, Mrs Stewart improved her speed to 135.95 mph, the ultimate Ladies' lap record. But no praise is too great for Mrs Petre — to lap at 134.75 mph was a feat of skill and bravery of the highest order, especially remembering that Cobb, who knew the old car so intimately, did his best lap at 133.88 mph, Bertram at 135.34 mph.

After the 1935 season the Delage was refused a licence to race, and its Brooklands days were over. It had been one of the most consistently successful cars to race there. However, VSCC members had a use for old racing cars and the V12 Delage accordingly appeared at that Club's Littlestone Speed Trials in 1937, driven by Gerald Sumner. It made ftd, in 22.6 sec.

Kay Petre setting off for some fast lappery in the Delage when it was owned by the JRDC.

In 1940 Cecil Clutton, while shopping for a Bugatti with Bill Shertt, found the great car in a sorry state at Street & Duller's premises in London, and purchased it along with a load of rusty spare parts. The arrangements to allow Kay Petre to drive it were still in place. The war and flying for the RAF then called a halt, and a fire in the barn in which the Delage was stored did not improve its condition. However, most wars end eventually, and after Sam (Clutton) had returned to civilian life his thoughts turned at once to the old racing car, which he was by then sharing with Peter Vaughan, who was still in Germany. A thorough restoration was obviously required, which was entrusted to Alan Southon at his Phoenix Green Garage in Hartley Wintney, just by the pub that was headquarters to the VSCC. It was found that in the engine of the Delage the centre main-bearing housing had four cracks in it, the dewel-pin retaining the bearing cage had broken free, and the crankcase was full of hairline cracks. Fortunately, the spare crankcase had come with the car, although with the hole made when a rod had escaped in the 1931 Gold Star race when Cobb was on a lower than his normal axle ratio. Alan made a fine job of plating this hole, but encountered great difficulty replacing with a new section of pipe that which, cast into the crankcase, had been flattened in the blow-up; but the job was done, work having commenced in January 1947. Clutton decided to have the wheels rebuilt to take 19 in. x 7 in. Dunlop tyres, the largest racing ones then available, but this, although allowing them to be changed round between the four wheels, proved to be a mistake, because the heavy covers rather changed the steering characteristics. A new radiator core was fitted and the two six-cylinder magnetos overhauled. The work was completed by July 1949, the body now in blue paint again.

The Delage was taken to Silverstone for testing. After initially refusing to run, it then ran badly, oiling-up the plugs. New piston rings were installed in 1949 and the trouble vanished. The Delage was then taxed for the road, for the first time in its life, detachable mudguards made by Alan being able to stand up to speeds of 115 mph. Clutton always drove the big car to race meetings, and I recall one run with him from Hartley Wintney to Silverstone when he went to 110 mph in third gear and nudged perhaps 130 mph in top. As Vaughan had been posted to Malaya, Forrest Lycett took over the part share in this exciting motor car. At VSCC Silverstone in 1950, having driven there alone, Sam won his class in the half-mile sprint, in 26 seconds, beaten only by the Norris Special.

The engine of the 10¹/₂-litre V12 Delage, showing the four downdraught carburettors. This is a Guy Griffiths photograph.

The Delage, nearest to the camera, lining up for a sprint race at Brooklands.

Another view of the same sprint event, in 1934. The other cars are: No. 6 Oats's Maserati, No. 5 Dick Nash's Anzani-Nash, No. 2 Tom Delaney's Lea-Francis, with Thomas Fotheringham's Bugatti behind. Oliver Bertram won this scratch race in the Delage (No. 1) from the Maserati, covering the (approximately) 700 yards at 73.10 mph. The car was at that time painted blue, with black wheels.

At a later race meeting there was a pin-hole leak in one of the very thin forged-steel cylinder barrels (the engine then had 12 separate cylinders) filled the sump with water. A spare barrel was fitted but came adrift on the next outing, a calamity which all-night work cured. The brakes had been found to be very poor indeed, in spite of the Alfin drums, and although a 40/50 hp Delage mechanical servo was found, and the 10½-litre had provision for a gearbox-driven servo, the design of that for the standard chassis was different and would not adapt. So the non-servo Perrot four-wheel brakes with masses of pulleys, which Sam referred to as 'compensating nonsense', remained. The 1950 season ended with Southon driving the Delage against Lycett's legendary 8-litre Bentley (another car in which I have had rapid rides) at the Brighton Speed Trials, and was only about 30 yards behind at the finish, going over the line at 118 mph.

That season the car still had a 7-to-1 compression ratio, and was run on the only surviving axle ratio of 2.18-to-1. (Originally there was a choice of seven ratios of from 1.95 to 3.36 to 1, giving overall ratios of 6.75, 4.02, 2.73 and 2.18 to 1), representing approximately 107 mph at 3,000 rpm. Sam would have preferred something nearer 2.4-to-1 in top. The four Zenith-downdraught carburettor system, fitted by Robin Jackson in 1931, was still in use but the two old updraught double-choke Zeniths and their long manifolds came with the car. Starting, even from cold, was easy, as the starting-handle was geared down 6½-to-1, a geared-up starting-magneto was driven from the same gear-train, and a Kigass was also fitted.

The 10½-litre Delage in its Silverstone days, photographed by Guy Griffiths. Cecil Clutton is in the driver's seat, whilst Holland Birkett (with sign in hand) and Forrest Lycett, on his left, look on. Alan Southon (bare-headed), who worked on the car, stands behind it.

After all these giant racing cars in this and the companion Aero-Engined Racing Cars at Brooklands, *here is something at the opposite extreme — the 348 cc Blackburne-engined Gush Special, renamed the Vitesse Special, which in 1934 set the Class J one-hour record to 73.04 mph.*

Clutton put up some excellent performances with the car — its successes including winning the 1951 season VSCC Vintage Trophy Race, at 72.31 mph. Alas, in one of these races, in 1952, a cylinder broke away, setting the car well and truly on fire. Clutton had to vacate the cockpit and let the car dive into the Woodcote ditch — he was flung off, already considerably burned. At the time, my 1926 15.9 hp Delaunay-Belleville was parked to the left of Woodcote Corner; so I was particularly grateful that Clutton did not use that line of escape! It took Cecil Clutton some time in hospital to recover, and his hands showed the effects of the fire.

It seemed that the Delage might never run again. However, it was not all that badly damaged, and in 1965/66 Hoffmann & Burton, the vintage Bentley specialists of Henley-on-Thames, took it in hand. The engine was rebuilt, with two cylinder blocks in place of the separate cylinders with their welded-on water jackets; the four downdraught Zenith carburettors were retained. The car was soon back on the vintage competition scene, shared by Jack Williamson and Clutton and after Clutton's death Jack Williamson continued to run it. Today the old Delage still makes welcome appearances, driven by Jack or his son Johnty.

Appendix 1

BARC Rules and Regulations

**THE RULES AND REGULATIONS ISSUED BY
THE BROOKLANDS AUTOMOBILE RACING CLUB**

REGULATIONS

TO BE OBSERVED BY PERSONS USING THE
BROOKLANDS MOTOR COURSE

1 The admission of motor cars, drivers, and occupants, and of motor-cycles, is conditional upon the observance of all the following regulations; their violation may entail exclusion, either temporary or permanent.
2 The charge for the use of the Course is 10s. per car per day, except in the case of members, subscribers, or those having tickets. For motor-cycles the charge is 5s. per motor-cycle per day.
3 No dogs are admitted to the grounds.
4 Motor cars must be shod with india-rubber tyres, and their axle weight must not exceed 2,700 lbs. Cars fitted with tyres having metal studs or projections may, at the discretion of the officials, be precluded from using the Track.
5 All cars must be fitted either with a first receiver close to the engine, and an exhaust pipe therefrom reaching as far as the back axle, or with an exhaust pipe and efficient silencer. *Cut-outs or like contrivances must not be used on the Motor Course*, and cars fitted with same may be excluded at the discretion of the officials.
6 Sirens, horns, or whistles must not be used on the Motor Course, or on the private road leading thereto, and no motor car shall create unnecessary noise.
7 Admission of motor cars and motor-cycles will entitle them to drive a left-handed course round the oval part of the Track, at all speeds. *Cars and motor-cycles must not be driven at high speeds in the Straight,* and must not pass the Paddock to re-enter the oval part of the Track. For this purpose cars and motor-cycles must re-enter the Paddock from the Straight and depart therefrom by the exit gate.
8 No race with another motor car or motor-cycle is to be carried out without the official in charge of the Paddock having been notified, and having made the necessary arrangements for such race taking place without danger to other users of the Track.
9 *No motor car or motor-cycle shall be stopped on the Track.* Should temporary adjustments become necessary, the car or cycle must first be dri-

ven to one of the refuges before it is stopped. Persons infringing this regulation *are liable to a fine of* 10s., and, failing payment, may be excluded.

10 No occupant of a motor car shall alight from the car on to the Track; he must await the car being in a refuge before he alights. *No person shall walk on the Track.* Persons *standing in a refuge* shall not *cross the line dividing the refuge from the main Track.* Persons infringing this regulation *shall be liable to a fine of* 10s., and, failing payment, may be excluded.

11 Drivers are requested not to drive wide, that is to say, they are asked to drive as close to the inner edge of the Track as the speed at which they are travelling will admit without a side-strain being put upon their wheels.

12 If any obstruction be met on the Track (and a car travelling in the same direction or an official car travelling in the opposite direction, as specified under 13, shall be deemed an obstruction) the driver shall steer to the right, and pass it by, leaving it on his left-hand side.

13 Officials will at times proceed round the Track in a right-hand direction (contrary to the direction prescribed for drivers), either on foot, cycle, or motor car. They will invariably keep close to the inner edge of the Track. Other users of the Track must not, in any circumstances, drive in a right-handed direction.

14 Drivers are requested to slow down when a yellow flag is shown on the Track, to stop near the official who has hoisted it, and follow his instructions.

15 For the purpose of entering the Track, every motor car or motor-cycle shall first be driven to the Paddock, and from there shall reach the Track by such gate as may be directed by the official in charge.

16 The officials have orders to see that the regulations are strictly adhered to, and users of the Course will greatly assist the management, and do much to ensure their own and others' safety, by readily submitting to the directions of the officials.

17 All complaints should be addressed either to the official in charge of the Paddock or to the Clerk of the Course.

DRIVING TOO HIGH ON THE BANKING
STEWARDS' CIRCULAR OF 11TH JULY, 1912

DEAR SIR,

It has been observed by the Stewards at recent race meetings that a good many cars, when racing at speeds of from 70 to 80 miles an hour, go very high up on the banking, especially on the Byfleet side of the Track, near the Aviation Sheds, with the result that cars of superior speeds are unable to pass above them without getting too high themselves.

I am instructed to remind you that not only is there a danger of skidding down the banking when a car is being driven unnecessarily high, and that the forcing of other cars higher still puts them in a similar danger, but also if a car is driven at a point on the banking which is higher than the natural line, the way of the car is stopped owing to the amount of steering which is required to keep it from skidding, and, of course, the circuit of the Track is slightly increased in length.

The centre line of the Track, that is to say, the black dotted line, has been calculated as being the normal position for a car running at a speed of 60 miles an hour, and by experiment it can be ascertained which is the proper course to take at speeds exceeding or less than this.

Now that the handicappers have been able to gauge with much greater accuracy the speed of cars, and therefore to bring them nearer together on the finishing line, there is a tendency for cars to gather together on the Byfleet banking at the last circuit, and consequently it is essential, if the best sport is to be obtained, that each car should, as far as practicable, keep on the course most suited to its speed.

Yours faithfully,
F. LINDSAY LLOYD,
Clerk of the Course

FURTHER INSTRUCTIONS TO DRIVERS, 1926

A black dotted line has been painted 10 feet in from the outer edge of the Track.

Cars should normally drive sufficiently below this line so as to leave room on their right for a car to pass them without crossing the line.

In no case may a car cross the line unless the driver has first satisfied himself that by so doing he will not obstruct a faster car coming up behind him.

F. LINDSAY LLOYD,
Clerk of the Course

INSTRUCTIONS TO DRIVERS FOR PULLING UP
AT COMPLETION OF RACES FINISHING IN THE
FINISHING STRAIGHT

(These regulations are issued in order that drivers may not only themselves know what they are expected to do after passing the Finishing Line, but also may be certain what others behind or in front of them may be expected to do. Strict attention to these regulations will diminish any risk of collision to a negligible amount.)

1 The Finishing Line will be varied according to the speed of the cars or cycles taking part in a race, the condition of the Track, etc.
    It will be indicated by a double black line painted across the Track and a row of small flags suspended above this line.
    Drivers will make themselves acquainted, before leaving the Paddock for a race, of the position of the Finishing Line for that race.
2 Apply brakes and shut off power immediately on passing the Finishing Line.
3 After passing Finishing Line, bear towards the inner edge of Track, and endeavour to reduce speed to between 20 and 30 miles an hour prior to reaching the left-hand bend connecting Finishing Straight with main Track. Remember that other cars may be close behind you, and therefore make no sudden turn or alteration of course.
4 A broad black line is painted on the concrete, forming a curve, commencing in the last 50 yards of the pull up, and leading into the main Track. This line, called the "Limit Line", should in no circumstances be crossed by drivers when pulling up.
5 Having entered the main Track, after making the left-hand turn, continue to decrease speed (still bearing towards the inner edge of the

Track) until, after passing the subway, you cross a broad black line painted on the concrete at right angles to the direction of the main Track (called the "Stopping Line").

6   No car or cycle should in any circumstances come to a stand prior to having passed the above-mentioned Stopping Line; any driver disregarding this instruction will be liable to disqualification.

7   After passing the Stopping Line, drivers should turn in at the gate, but should not cross the Limit Line before doing so. Any driver crossing the Limit Line will render himself liable to disqualification, it being conclusive proof that he was travelling at an excessive speed, or that his car or cycle was not under proper control when crossing the Stopping Line.

When races finish on the Circuit of the Track cars will continue the circuit and enter the Paddock by proceeding down the Finishing Straight. It is very desirable that Winning Cars should enter the Straight and Paddock in the order of finishing.

GENERAL

BRAKES

One of the two independent brakes required by "The Motor Cars (Use and Construction) Order, 1904" must operate on the driving wheels of a car so that speed of such a car can be checked, even if the propeller-shaft or driving-chains shall have carried away.

[In 1931 this was revised to read: 'Every car in a race must have at least one effective braking system and this must operate even if the transmission of the car shall fail.']

ENGINE CONTROL

Every car shall be fitted with an ignition switch so placed that the driver can at any moment cut off the ignition and so stop the engine without difficulty.

BONNET STRAPS

Every car provided with a bonnet must have a leather strap not less than 1 $\frac{1}{2}$ inches wide and $\frac{1}{8}$ inch thick, firmly secured at both ends and passing right round the centre of the bonnet.

IN RACING TRIM

Means a car without any touring accessories, such as hood, screens, lamps, etc. If mudguards and running-boards form an integral part of the construction of the chassis, this must be stated on the entry form, otherwise the handicappers — in a handicap race — will assume they have been removed.

FUEL

Except where specially provided in the race proposition, any fuel which is commercially obtainable may be used in internal combustion engines, and the oxygen required for combustion must be obtained directly from the atmosphere. Any infraction of this regulation shall be deemed a corrupt practice, and dealt with accordingly.

EXHAUSTS

1   An ordinary touring car or cycle must be fitted with an ordinary tour-

ing silencer if and when used on the Track for private and touring purposes as distinct from competitions.

2 Except as above mentioned all cars and motor-cycles when running on the Track shall be fitted with the type of silencer hereinafter described.

3 *Construction.* –

(*a*) A pipe leading from the exhaust valve or valves shall be led into a receiver which shall be situated as close as possible to the engine.

(*b*) This pipe shall penetrate into the receiver to a distance of two inches, and no more.

(*c*) The capacity of the receiver mentioned in paragraph (a) shall not be less than six times the volume swept by the piston of one cylinder of the engine, and such receiver, if cylindrical, shall not be of greater length than four times its maximum diameter, and if of irregular shape of equivalent proportions.

(*d*) An exit pipe shall lead from this cylinder as far as the back axle. This exit pipe shall protrude into the receiver specified in paragraph (*a*) to a depth of two inches, and no part of this exit pipe shall be of greater cross-sectional area than the minimum area of the exhaust port of any one cylinder.

(*e*) The pipes leading into and out of the receiver shall not be opposite each other in the receiver, but shall be out of line to the extent of one-and-a-half inches measured at points on the circumference, and not between pipe centres, so that if the pipes were continued there would be a space between the pipes at a place where they overlapped sufficient to allow of the passage of a one-and-a-half-inch gauge.

(*f*) No device may be employed in the receiver which would tend to produce a straight-through flow of the exhaust gases between the inlet and outlet pipes.

(*g*) The exhaust gases must not pass direct from the exit pipe to the atmosphere but must all be finally emitted from what is commonly known as a "fish-tail" on the end of the exit pipe. The orifice of such "fish tail" shall be approximately rectangular in shape, and of the following dimensions: —

	Small dimension Not more than	Large dimension Not less than
For engines with a capacity up to and including two litres	$1/4$ in.	6 in.
Over two litres	$1/2$ in.	12 in.

The length of the fish-tail when fitted shall be measured from the end of the exit pipe to a point situated at the centre of the orifice, and the length of the fish-tail shall be equal to the large dimension of the orifice. Thus, if the orifice of the fish-tail is 9 inches by $1/4$ inch, the distance from the end of the exit pipe (where the tail commences) to the centre of the orifice shall be 9 inches.

The surfaces of the fish-tail shall be flattened as far as possible, and shall taper from the end of the exit pipe to the orifice.

(*h*) The after-half of the sides of the fish-tail, that is to say, the half of the fish-tail nearest the orifice, may be perforated with holes not greater than $3/32$ inch in diameter. The number of holes is not limited.

4 In spite of the fact that a competitor may have complied with the above regulations the Brooklands Automobile Racing Club, through its official or duly appointed representative, shall have the right at any time to exclude any vehicle from the Track or grounds within its jurisdiction if in the opinion of such official or representative such vehicle has made or might make undue noise.

5 If while any vehicle is using the Track during the progress of a race, record-breaking attempt or test, or for any purpose whatever, its silencer should become detached, deranged or broken in such a manner as to allow of the emission of the exhaust gases through any other place than the orifice of the fish-tail, such vehicle shall, if competing in any race, record-breaking attempt or test, be liable from that moment to be disqualified from taking any further part in any such event, and shall in any case throttle down and leave the Track forthwith.

6 The Brooklands Automobile Racing Club by its official or duly appointed representative reserves the right to examine the interior of any silencing apparatus fitted on competing vehicles, and may disqualify any competitor whose apparatus in the opinion of such official or representative does not comply with these regulations, and may withhold, withdraw or deal with as it thinks fit, any prize, certificate or other award to which such competitor would otherwise have become entitled as a result of the use of the offending vehicle.

NO ADVERTISEMENTS TO BE CARRIED WITHOUT CONSENT OF CLUB

No advertisement or trade sign shall be carried on or be distributed from any vehicle during any competition, except with the special consent of the Club first obtained.

CROSSING AND PASSING

A competitor who crosses another in any part of a race so as to interfere with that or any other competitor's chance, is liable to disqualification, unless it be proved that he was two clear vehicle-lengths ahead before taking ground in front of his opponent.

LEAVING THE COURSE

Any competitor leaving the course shall, if he desires, return to and continue the contest from the point where he left the course.

RESTARTING—NO OUTSIDE ASSISTANCE

No vehicle, while competing, shall be pushed, aided, or set in motion by any persons other than the driver and his assistant, if an assistant be carried.

CONTROLS

If any control shall be established for the purpose of limiting speed and for which a time limit shall be prescribed, any competitor who shall pass through such control without having stopped until the prescribed period has elapsed shall be penalised with a number of minutes equal to three times the time of the control, unless he be able to furnish proof to the satisfaction of the Stewards that the checking officials had not arrived or were not at their post, in which case the matter shall be dealt with in accordance with the regulations applying to the competition.

COMPETITORS' ENCLOSURE
The officials of the meeting shall have power to limit admission to the Competitors' Enclosure to competitors, their drivers and assistants (one to each driver).

COMPETITORS MUST BE REGISTERED
No competitor shall be eligible to enter a vehicle for or drive a vehicle in any competition unless the name of such competitor is duly entered upon the Competitors' Register of the Automobile Club. The competitor shall produce the certificate of registration of the Automobile Club on the demand of an official of the Club at any meeting.

FEE
The fee for such registration of a competitor is half-a-guinea, except in the case of a member of the Automobile Club or of a Club affiliated to the Automobile Club, in which case the fee is five shillings.

REGISTER NUMBER
Each entry in the Register is given a Register Number, which holds good until the 31st day of December next ensuing.

EXTRA FEE FOR ASSUMED NAME
On payment of an additional annual fee of two guineas a competitor may be registered under an assumed name approved by the Automobile Club; provided that the competitor while registered under such assumed name shall not compete under any other name.

NUMBERING OF VEHICLES
Every entrant shall provide and fix at his own expense, on some part of his vehicle behind the driver's seat, a metal disc, painted black; this disc shall be fixed in a vertical plane, corresponding with the longitudinal axis of the vehicle, and must be plainly visible at right angles on its whole extent, which shall not be less than 2 feet in height and 2 feet in length.

DRIVERS
Every driver or mechanic taking part in any race shall be a male person, unless the race proposition expressly states otherwise.

POWER OF CLERK OF THE COURSE
The Clerk of the Course may, subject to an appeal to the Stewards, cause the removal from a competing vehicle of any appliance which might give a competitor an undue advantage during a race.

Appendix 2

The 1907 Montagu Cup Race

This, the first race of any distance to be run at the newly-opened Brooklands Track on 6 July 1907, can be said to have been a race of giants, although not all the cars necessarily had engines exceeding a capacity of 10-litres. The most important event of the Track's inaugural afternoon, the first prize amounted to 1,400 sovereigns, plus the Cup presented by Lord Montagu of Beaulieu, father of the present Lord Montagu of National Motor Museum fame.

The rules specified cars with engines up to 155 x 235 mm; steam cars barred. The distance was 30.456206 miles — the BARC was that precise. This made the race the longest on the card, the next longest being the 15.75-mile Gottlied Daimler Memorial Plate. Presumably in the hope of attracting entries, the BARC had issued a list of eligible chassis, of which many of the racing cars would be based. This list ran from 40 hp Darracq to 130 hp Dietrich and Panhard — 34 in all. Total prize money was 2,100 sovereigns. The weight of each car was restricted to 2,600 lb.

In fact, only eight entries were received, comprising the 1906 14.5-litre Grand Prix Mercedes of J. E. Hutton and F. R. Fry, the latter to be driven by the famous Dario Resta, Prince Okura of Japan on his noisy 120 hp Fiat, Warwick Wright's Darracq, a 90 hp Napier entered by S. F. Edge for Cecil Edge to drive, G. Baxendale's Darracq, H. R. Pope's Itala, with M. Fabry up, and another Mercedes which F. Rendle had put in for A. G. Brown to conduct.

From the start Hutton led but the better acceleration of the Napier gave it the advantage, lower on the banking, as they took the Members' turn. The Mercedes, however, hung on well, but it was Warwick Wright's Darracq that was soon in its stride and rushing after the leaders. He was second at the end of the second lap, and in the lead on the third lap. Now, though, Resta had Fry's Mercedes running effectively and he was third as three laps were completed. The rest were a long way behind. So the battle was between Darracq, Napier and Mercedes, with the French car seeming the likely winner. Then, on lap 4, the Napier developed engine trouble and dropped out — Edge's feelings no doubt indescribable. Those who had put money on the Napier could not have been very happy either, because it was the favourite at 2 to 1.

The fifth lap was exciting because, while the Darracq looked to be uncatchable, Hutton's Mercedes had closed on it a little, and Resta was now a close third. Nothing is certain in motor racing, however, and on lap 8, with three more to complete, the Darracq slowed, and on the next circuit stopped with serious damage — the crankcase holed and the camshaft bent. Now it was all up to the two Mercedes, but Hutton's had a cylinder out of action, so Resta, who had played a waiting game on the fast and punishing Brooklands Track, had only to drive up the Finishing Straight to take that 1,400 sovereigns and the valuable Montagu Cup. Alas, for him, he failed to see the horse-race style semaphore signal at the Fork, indicating that he should bear left, and he continued for another circuit, giving the race to Hutton. The 120 hp Fiat of Prince Okura finished third. Resta claimed to have counted his laps correctly, but had seen a man waving him on round the banking. The BARC preferred not to listen ....

It may have been confusing for the onlookers at their first British track race, but at least they had seen the winner average some 82 mph, and the Napier and Darracq, before they retired, go past at well over 90 mph. The other Darracq had tyre trouble.

The majority of the spectators may have failed to understand what had happened, but the Giants had been released . . .

Appendix 3

The Origin of the Tipo S61 Fiat

After Anthony Heal had discovered the giant four-cylinder 130 × 190 mm (10,087 cc) Fiat which had raced with considerable success at Brooklands (Chapter 11) there was some discussion as to its identity and whether it had or had not started life as a genuine racing car. The problem was put to the celebrated motoring writer and historian Kent Karslake, whose articles in pre-war issues of *Motor Sport* had spurred on the VSCC to introduce its class for pre-1915 "Edwardian" motor cars, and which was to unearth those great racing monsters from the past. Karslake tackled the problem of the 10-litre Fiat in his inimitable and thorough manner as follows:

I set to work to discover something about the car. I genuinely did remember it well enough in its post-war Brooklands days, but as to its origin I was completely in the dark.

One thing was fairly easy to establish, namely that from 1910 or 1911 until 1914 the F.I.A.T. company listed the Type S61, with four cylinders of 130 × 190 mm bore and stroke, as its standard 90 hp model. Moreover the factory weighed in with the information that the Tipo S61 was made in 1910. It would therefore have been fairly easy to reach the conclusion that this car was No. 42 of a standard series and to leave it at that.

It did not, however, seem very satisfactory to leave it at that. In the first place there was a sneaking reluctance to admit that the machine was not a genuine racing-car; and moreover, even in the spacious days of before the war, it was rather unusual to design a 10-litre standard model without any particular excuse. So research continued.

It strayed to the annals of the first Grand Prize of America, which was run as a road race in 1911, and in which a F.I.A.T. finished third. Investigation proved that this machine, according to a contemporary report, had a bore and stroke of 5 × 7½ inches, which, converted at 25.4 mm = inch, gives an equivalent of 127 × 191 mm, as near as may be. There were no engine size regulations for the race, and the dimensions therefore were probably given to the nearest quarter inch. On this assumption it was fairly obvious that we were dealing with our old friend the 130 × 190 mm engine.

But this did not really help matters much. If the engine was standardised in 1910 it obviously could not have been designed for a race in 1911. Moreover it would have been very surprising in those days if a European manufacturer had gone to the trouble of designing a car for an American race, which they usually won with a racer several years old. I began to search for an earlier European race.

The last French Grand Prix, in 1908, had produced F.I.A.T.s with much bigger bores—155 mm was the limit for the race and the Italian firm built up to it. The next French Grand Prix, in 1912, was a free-for-all race, and the F.I.A.T.s which ran in it had a relatively long stroke, but not such a big stroke-bore ratio as our problem car. For my own edification I produced a little table, as follows: –

GRAND PRIX F.I.A.T.s

	Regulations	Bore & Stroke	Stroke-Bore Ratio
1906	Weight limit	180 x 160 mm	0.90:1
1907	Fuel consumption limit	180 x 160 mm	0.90:1
1908	Bore limited to 155 mm	155 x 160 mm	1.03:1
1912	Free-for-all	150 x 200 mm	1.33:1
?	?	130 x 190 mm	1.46:1

The big increase in the stroke-bore ratio between 1908 and 1912 suggested that in the meantime the factory had had experience of long-stroke engines, but that probably this experience had been forced on its designers by the limited bore rule. One must obviously seek for a race with such regulations to find the origin of the design.

At this point a red herring was drawn across the path. A High Authority volunteered the information that "the car is probably the 90 hp Taunus model." What did this mean? The only significance this had for me was that the Kaiserpreis race of 1907 was run over the Taunus Circuit. But the dimensions of the F.I.A.T.s which ran in this race were given as 140 x 130 mm, and besides the rules limited the capacity to 8-litres. The discovery of a standard model F.I.A.T. for 1909 called the 90 hp Taunus type with a bore and stroke of 140 x 129 mm stopped further progress along this false trail.

After this I cast back to the Targa Florio, and found, not without some excitement, that the regulations for the 1908 race stipulated a maximum bore of 130 mm. But in a year in which F.I.A.T. for a Grand Prix, run to a bore limit of 155 mm, only dared use a stroke of 160 mm, one was unlikely to find any such exaggerated dimensions as 130 x 190; and in fact the 1908 Targa Florio F.I.A.T.s had a stroke of only 140 mm.

So far the search had centred exclusively on cars which ran in races. What about racing-cars which never ran? Here I am convinced was found at last the answer to the riddle. No French Grand Prix was run in 1909, but the regulations for the race were prepared, and they stipulated a maximum bore of 130 mm. Surely here is to be found the origin of the F.I.A.T. A jump in the stroke from 140 mm to 190 mm in one year, with the bore remaining at 130 mm, seems a big one. But serious consideration of the limited bore rule must have led to observation of the Voiturettes, where Peugeot in 1909 was using a stroke-bore ratio of 2.5:1. I am therefore fairly convinced that this F.I.A.T. design was made for the 1909 Grand Prix which never took place, and then used *faute de mieux* as a standard model in 1910, eventually becoming a racing design again on the occasion of the American Grand Prize in 1911.

Having reached this point I was still keen to prove that the particular car in question was a real racing-car built for the 1909 Grand Prix. I was not much worried by the date, because when the race was called off, they might well not have troubled to finish the cars before 1910. But I was worried by "No. 42". I even tried out a theory that all F.I.A.T. rac-ing-cars were in a series S61, and I counted thirteen pre-1909 types as follows:—1900 "Padua" type; 1901 "Piombino-Grossetto"; 1902 "Mont Cenis"; 1903 Paris–Madrid; 1904 Gordon-Bennett; 1905 Gordon-Bennett; 1906 Targa Florio; 1906 Grand Prix; 1907 Targa Florio; 1907 Kaiserpreis; 1907 Grand Prix; 1908 Targa Florio and 1908 Grand Prix. Allowing three cars of each type this would make thirty-nine cars, and the third of the 1909 Grand Prix type would be No. 42! But this ingenu-ity failed to convince even myself.

At this point came a momentary thrill in the shape of information from a former owner that engine No. 42 (of date 1911) was not that orig-inally belonging to the chassis, although it was of the same type. But the consequent elation was short-lived as he added that the original engine was No. 25 (of date 1910). I think therefore that this particular machine cannot have started life as a racing-car, but must have belonged to the standard series.

A Battle of Giants

The final of the 1932 British Empire Trophy outer-circuit race which the British Racing Drivers' Club put on at Brooklands was one of the most exciting and hard fought battles of the giants ever seen at the Track. It was contested over 36 laps, or 100 miles, but unfortunately was marred by protests.

The starters included Sir Henry Birkin with the lap-record-holding blower 4$\frac{1}{2}$-litre Bentley single-seater, John Cobb in the old but formidable 10$\frac{1}{2}$-litre V12 Delage, experienced George Eyston with the 8-litre single-seater Panhard Levassor, and Jack Dunfee in Woolf Barnato's 6$\frac{1}{2}$-litre Speed Six Track Bentley. A battle of giants was in prospect, and no-one was disappointed, speaking for the spectators that is.

In fact, this turned out to be one of the closest very fast races ever seen. It was won by Cobb in the big Delage at 126.363 mph. He was just $\frac{2}{10}$ ths of a second ahead of Capt. G. E. T. Eyston in the Panhard, after some of the most intense motor racing imaginable. So close were they that the difference in race average speed was a mere 0.009 mph. Eyston protested that he had been baulked and was given the verdict. Cobb counter-protested to the RAC and was later awarded first place. (These drivers won the Empire Trophy and £100, and £50, respectively.) At that time I said I found that decision satisfactory. Now, with hindsight, and having before me the official lap-by-lap times for this remarkable race, it seems opportune to take a fresh look at what occurred down at Weybridge on that eventful 30 April 1932.

The BRDC's Secretary, H. N. Edwards, and its race sub-committee usually chaired by Lord Howe, thought more entries would have been acceptable and the closing date was extended, at the existing fee of £11 per car. The prizes were donated by Sir Harold Bowden, and Edwards had taken upon himself to name those for the heats, the South Africa, India, Canada and Australia trophies. He had used HRH Prince George's name in Press hand-outs, and later the Prince stated that he had no objection. (It was hoped that the Prime Minister might be invited to take some part in the forthcoming BRDC 500 Mile Race.)

From the beginning there was anxiety about the very fast cars involved being subject to overtaking problems. The faster of them were required to keep to the left of the black line at the Fork, except when overtaking, as laid down by the BARC itself in 1931. Drivers in the BE Trophy race were required to sign the back of the final Race Instructions to show they understood this rule. Eyston, however, wrote "Disagree entirely with regulation black line, want to ignore this, otherwise don't start", which has a significant bearing on the protests which were to follow.

Eyston did start, of course, so was persuaded to ignore his objection. Why did he express it? He had raced at Brooklands but more recently had used Montlhéry Track, whereas his chief rival John Cobb was extremely well versed in lapping very fast round Brooklands, having started with the aged 10-litre Fiat in 1925 and holding the Class A lap-record at over 132 mph with the Delage.

It seems to me that Eyston was aware that the 10½-litre V12 Delage could out-accelerate the 8-litre Panhard, a not-much-younger car (which proved to be the case) and that if he kept to the left of the Fork black line and Cobb passed him, he would never be able to catch the bigger-engined car. Or it may be, perhaps a subsidiary thought, that Eyston feared he would lose too much pace and concentration if he had to so place the heavy-handling Panhard when pulling it off the Byfleet banking as to keep the black line to his offside.

This BE Trophy Race was obviously between the two Bentleys, the Delage and the Panhard, Earl Howe's 1½-litre GP Delage and Widengren's 1½-litre OM being outclassed.

Thanks to help from the BRDC archives, we are able to analyse what happened, lap by lap. A. V. Ebblewhite signed the time-sheets, so they can be regarded as infallible, while laps were timed to the nearest ⅕th of a second. If drivers did cross a forbidden line (but see earlier) or were thought to be baulking another car, they were to be shown a black flag bearing a white cross, and all signal flags were to be a uniform size.

As the starting flag fell, Cobb accelerated away and led the first lap by four seconds from Eyston. Birkin then got the blower Bentley into its stride and overtook Eyston, to lead the race at the end of lap 4. This continued until, with a bang which was mistaken for a burst tyre, the Bentley cracked its cylinder block and retired on lap 18, when 4.6 sec. ahead of Eyson. So far as the Eyston/Cobb duel went, the Delage kept ahead of the Panhard for the first six laps, by margins of 4, 4.8, 3.2, 1.6, 0.8 and 0.6 sec. The Panhard then got past and ran in first place for the next 19 laps. The margins varied as follows: 1.0 sec. on lap 7, then by 1.2, 2.6, 3.6, 3.2, 2.4, 3.0, 2.4, 1.8, 1.2, 2.2, 1.4, 1.0, 2.6, 2.6, 3.8, 1.8, 1.4 and 0.4 sec. (One wonders if the slower time on lap 22 may have been caused by Eyston weighing up the position after realising that Birkin was out, or wanting to conserve his tyres?)

Cobb had said he would not open right out until about five laps from the finish and Eyston was known to be troubled about the life of the Panhard's tyres. Eyston may have eased off a fraction, because the Delage slipped past on the inside as they entered the Railway Straight, to lead by 0.8 sec. at the end of lap 26. Its lead dropped to 0.6 sec. on the next circuit and then the Delage, rather earlier than intended, was opened up, to lead by 1.6 and 1.2 sec.

However, Eyston had clearly seen the danger and put the Panhard in fierce pursuit. He closed to within 0.4 sec. on the following two laps and from lap 31 to the finish line he had the Panhard within a mere 0.2 sec. of the Delage on every lap; but he was unable to overtake.

Driving these big racing cars at over 130 mph so close to each other and very near the unprotected banking edge, knowing that if the car in front got ever so slightly out of control they had virtually no brakes with which to cope — and there was also the ever-present risk of tyre bursts (in fact, Eyston lost a tyre tread immediately after the race had ended) —called for considerable bravery.

It must have been some spectacle, these two giant cars lapping to within a lap-time of $\frac{1}{5}$th of a second of one another, for those final furious six laps. Eyston had done his best, attempting to pull his heavy car early off the Byfleet banking in the hope of taking the Delage on the inside across the Fork. To no avail. Nor had he the surplus acceleration to overtake Cobb along the half-mile of the Railway Straight. But far from leaving his challenge to the last six laps, Cobb confessed he had had to drive flat-out for the final 12 laps or so, catching and passing the Panhard but thereafter keeping it only slightly in arrears. (Eyston's minor changes in times on laps 28 and 29 were probably the result of his unsuccessful bids on awkward lines to pass the Delage.)

Whatever your verdict of the outcome of the two protests is, you must surely agree it had been a magnificent track race. Earl Howe thought it the best yet. It must have rivalled the fine display of aerobatics in a Fairey Firefly 11M which F/Lt Chris Staniland had given before the race commenced! We now know that Eyston protested verbally at his inability to pass the Delage, saying he had been baulked, while still sitting in the Panhard, immediately after finishing. He was informed that such a protest could only be accepted in writing, accompanied by the requisite £5 fee. Now Eyston was one of the most gentlemanly of racing drivers and no doubt that spoken comment was the reaction of a very tired and disappointed man. I understand that Eyston did not want to take any further steps. But friends, including Kaye Don, apparently pointed out that the Panhard had been brought over from France for the purpose of winning this well-publicised race and that as a professional driver, if he thought he should have won, Eyston should protest. So he did!

The Stewards called both drivers before them, debated for two and a half hours, and found in favour of George Eyston. John Cobb then put in a counter protest to the RAC and a proper legal hearing was instituted.

My comments? The Observer called to hear Eyston's protest agreed with the Stewards that it should be upheld, and during Heat 4 the blue flag had twice been shown to Cobb, who was deemed to be preventing Dunfee from overtaking, it being recommended that the Clerk of the Course speak to the driver, at his discretion.

It took Dunfee seven laps to get by, although he got within 0.2 seconds of Cobb. It might also be noted that in this 18-lap heat Eyston passed Cobb on lap two, to lead throughout, winning at 126.21 mph, Cobb settling for third place after both Birkin and Dunfee had passed him, Birkin later falling back. But nothing conclusive there, except that the Panhard was nearly a minute ahead of the Dunfee Bentley at the finish, as Cobb may not have been trying. (Cobb had a mere 0.2 sec. lead after that first lap, and was three seconds in arrears after the next lap.) Eyston made fastest lap, at 131.41 mph, quicker than Parry Thomas's old Class B speed.

The race itself involved another protest, when Dunfee was crawling round on the last lap with a burst tyre and was inadvertently flagged into the Finishing Straight instead of over the Fork finishing line, giving third place to Howe's little Delage. The Stewards found that there was no proper liaison between the finish line officials and the parking officials but that the driver should have continued until seeing the prescribed finish flag. It was resolved by awarding Barnato and Dunfee consolation prizes.

The Cobb appeal became a legal battle. Lewis & Lewis, a leading firm of solicitors, instructed the Hon. Ewen Montague, KC, who had driven ABC,

Riley 9 and OM cars in MCC trials, to act for the Delage driver, assisted by Mr Brian Davis. Ernest Hancock represented Eyston. The BRDC Stewards, Sir Algernon Guinness, Lionel Martin and S. C. H. Davis, had well-known MCC member, trials driver and solicitor, D. Duncan-Smith, to look after their interests. The case was heard at the RAC before RAC Stewards Lord Cozens-Hardy, Sir Arthur Stanley, G. J. F. Knowles, H. B. Shackleton, Percy Short and Maurice Burton.

Unfortunately, the RAC no longer has the depositions, but apparently the Hon. Ewen Montague advanced the argument that as the drivers of the faster cars had agreed to pass, as far as possible, only on the Railway Straight (this in spite of all that fuss over the black line at the Fork!), Eyston had no sound reason to complain that he could not overtake the Delage on the banking. He made the further point that once Cobb was in the lead he had every right to choose his place for entering the Byfleet banking and could not be expected to ease up and wave his rival on.

It was also put forward that the Delage was the faster car, at which Eyston expressed surprise. The only evidence for this assumption seems to have been that eight years before the BE Trophy race, René Thomas had done a two-way mile at Arpajon at 143.31 mph and that Albert Divo was supposed to have lapped Montlhéry at 138.5 mph, at a time when the Delage was less highly tuned and had a lower compression ratio than it had by 1932, whereas when Eyston broke the Hour record at Montlhéry earlier that year, the Panhard's best lap was at 137 mph. There were those who said that as the V12 Delage had a capacity of 10,688 cc and weighted 34 cwt, against the Panhard-Levassor's 7,938 cc and 42 cwt, the Delage had been bound to win. Which overlooks the respective hp-per-litre of the engines, and the Panhard's better streamlining, etc. (Both drivers could be described, I think, as equally skilled and determined.) If the advantage possessed by the Delage was valid, it does seem somewhat odd that Cobb was satisfied to leave such a small margin between himself and Eyston for the final six laps of this very intense race.

The appeal lasted more than four hours, after which the RAC stewards took only ten minutes to award the race to Cobb. It was all settled amicably, with Eyston standing Cobb dinner afterwards. As usual, it was the public who suffered, because the hearing did not take place until 26 days after the race had been held — a long delay in deciding the outcome.

Montlhéry Track

Although all the cars described in this book were driven at Brooklands Track, the big Delage was driven by Albert Divo and Robert Benoist at Montlhéry, the Paris Autodrome, as recounted in Chapter 13. Brooklands had opened in 1907 but it was not until 1924 that the French, keen advocates of motor racing, built their banked motor course. The project was financed by M. Lamblin, whose profits came from his radiator manufacturing concern, but who was also the proprietor of the magazine *L'Aero Sports*.

Realising that a motor race track to which Parisians could flock might well be a profitable venture, M. Lamblin purchased a château standing in a 12,000 acre estate adjacent to the Paris–Orleans main road. It was here — between the villages of Linas-Montlhéry and Arpajon, where the speed trials were held, enabling Ernest Eldridge to put the World Land Speed Record to 146.01 mph on that narrow but straight piece of highway in 1924 (the last time this coveted fastest-of-all records was broken on a public road) — that Lamblin set about construction of what was to be named the Paris Autodrome.

Inexpensive labour, as at Brooklands, pushed the project along, and soon there arose two bankings, steeper even than those at Brooklands, joined by two short straights. The lap distance of the banked portion of the Montlhéry track (a long sinuous road circuit adjoined this and had access from it) was 1.6 miles or 2.5 km, compared to the 2.75 mile course in 360 acres of estate at Brooklands. Montlhéry's constructor had secured the services of a civil engineer, Raymond Jamin, rather as when contemplating the Brooklands Track on his Weybridge estate in Surrey, Hugh Fortescue Locke King employed the skills of Colonel Holden and a railway engineer named Donaldson.

The manager of the French construction work was M. Saint Macary, who had 2,000 men working in shifts, laying 35 metres of ferro-concrete per day. The château was made into a Clubhouse, and garages for the racing cars were built under the home banking. The Paddock was a large open surface of level concrete. The aim was to have the fastest track in the world, and the smooth surface of the new course and its very high bankings met that aim; although in the outcome there was not all that much difference in the absolute lap records set up to the outbreak of war at these two tracks — Montlhéry scoring by some 5 mph. As it was a flat-out course it was more tiring to compete on in the fastest racing cars than was Brooklands, where the Railway Straight half-mile provided drivers with some respite. Nor was the layout as attractive as that of Brooklands, which always retained its atmosphere of a well-kept English gentleman's country place. But there were no noise restrictions at Montlhéry, and it was accessible, being only 20 miles from Paris. It was opened on 4 October 1924. Today you will find it off National Route 20. Montlhéry is still in use, although alas rumours persist that its end may not be far distant.

Index